Praise for *Go Green, Live Rich*

"Great news: there is no green premium! By demonstrating how going green can fit any budget, David Bach shows that good environmental and financial decisions go hand-in-hand. Bach's *Go Green, Live Rich* gives great tips, useful to everyone, about how to save money and the planet at once. — ROBERT F. KENNEDY JR.

"Yet another powerful reason to go green! Thankfully for our species, going green can also mean saving some green. *Go Green, Live Rich* shows you exactly how a lot of small steps added together can change your life in more ways than one."
— GRAHAM HILL, TreeHugger.com and PlanetGreen.com

"I LOVE IT. LOVE IT. LOVE IT. This is just what the world needs. Not a bunch of touchy feely, mumbo jumbo, but real world solutions that show why going green is just plain smart. Fantastic."
— STEVE FLEISCHLI, President, Waterkeeper Alliance

"David Bach has done it again! As a green affordable housing developer, I enthusiastically recommend *Go Green, Live Rich*! Packed with tips and tools, this book is a must read for anyone who wants to make their home–and their life–more eco-friendly."
—JOSH LOCKWOOD,
Executive Director, Habitat for Humanity, New York City

"*Go Green, Live Rich* is as much about saving money as it is about preserving our world of natural wonders for future generations. This is the rich-green-book of a promising tomorrow."

— MATTHEW MODINE, Founder: Bicycle for a Day

"*Go Green, Live Rich* is the ultimate toolkit for greening the planet and our wallets at the same time. No one does a better job than David Bach in showing us the practical strategies for how to enjoy living sustainably."

—TERRY TAMMINEN, Cullman Senior Fellow, New America Foundation

"David Bach has created a truly easy-to-read, simple step-by-step plan for everyday consumers and business owners to make small changes towards achieving a greener way of life. From raising your baby to running your company, David shows you how to make positive changes on our planet as well as our bank accounts. Going green can definitely make everyone a little richer."

— BRADFORD RAND, President, Go Green Expo

"Finally, a book that debunks the myth that you have to BE rich to live green. In fact, it's the other way around: by living green you can GET rich – it's the ultimate win-win. Never before has this been spelled out so clearly, simply, practically. A must-read for anyone who wants to live wisely and responsibly in a world of rocketing energy prices and climate imbalance."   — AMANDA GRISCOM LITTLE,
    Award-winning environmental journalist and columnist for Grist.org

even more—up to 10,000 times more than tap water. And it's not necessarily purer water, since federal standards are higher for tap water than for bottled.

The backlash against "designer water" as a result of its environmental impact is growing. Cities like San Francisco have banned city employees from using tax dollars to purchase bottled water at work, and other cities are following suit.

Bottled-water companies are taking notice and working toward more environmentally friendly packaging and practices. Poland Spring, manufactured by Nestlé Waters, has introduced their new EcoShape bottle—which is 15 percent lighter and requires 10 to 15 percent less energy to make it. And FIJI Water recently announced "FIJI Green," an entire initiative to "protect and give back to the environment" with every bottle. These are improvements, but let's face it—the best solution is to carry your own tap water in a reusable container.

☐ Get a reusable water bottle and fill it with water from your tap. The newest generation of reusable water bottles, like those from SIGG (www.mysigg.com), are made of lightweight aluminum. And those from Klean Kanteen (www.kleankanteen.com) are made of stainless steel.

EnviroProducts manufactures a water bottle that is made from 100 percent corn grown in the United States. You can refill this bottle up to 90 times, and when you're done it biodegrades in just 80 days in a commercial compost! Check it out at www.newwaveenviro.com.

☐ If you have concerns about your tap water, it can easily and cheaply be filtered and purified. Visit www.waterfiltercomparisons.com to compare the leading brands and find one that's right for you.

2

DRIVE SMART,
FINISH RICH

N OTHING WILL CHANGE YOUR FINANCIAL future faster and improve the planet quicker than the decisions you make about what you drive and how you drive. Did you know that most Americans work two to four months a year just to pay for their car? In fact, car ownership is the second-highest household expense in the United States after shelter!

Not only that, but the car you drive is probably causing more damage to our planet than nearly anything else you do. How did we get here?

The truth is that America loves its cars. And the automotive industry spends around $14 billion a year to convince us, with undeniable success, to drive bigger, better, faster cars. We love our trucks even more. In fact, according to the National Automobile Dealers Association, 53 percent of vehicles on the road today are trucks (light trucks, vans, minivans, crossovers, and SUVs).

According to the Federal Highway Administration, there are 241 million cars and trucks on the road in the United States. That's 30 percent of the world's automobiles. And to power them, we use 8.2 million barrels of oil per day. That's almost as much oil as Saudi Arabia produces each day! It accounts for 11 percent of the world's daily oil consumption. All that fuel we burn in our cars fills the air with 1,300 million tons of CO_2 each year. That's seven tons per driver, or about 80 times that driver's body weight.

The impact on our planet is brutal. According to the United Nations Human Development Report released in November 2007, the automobile sector accounts for 30 percent of greenhouse gas emissions in developed countries—and that share is rising. Greenhouse gas emissions cause global warming—putting our planet, our futures, and life as we know it today in serious danger.

What can you do? Changing *what* you drive and *how* you drive it can save you a small fortune, clean up the air we breathe, and help to turn the tide on global warming.

Ready to get started?

GO GREEN
ACTION STEPS

☐ Find out what mileage you are currently getting. Visit the Environmental Protection Agency's *Green Vehicle Guide* at www.epa.gov/greenvehicles to look up your car model and see its highway and city fuel economy.

☐ Find a greener car. At www.greenercars.org, check out the listings of "greenest" cars (as well as the "meanest" ones). Decide which one you want to be driving.

Increase Your Fuel Economy

WHAT'S AMAZING TO ME IS THAT, DESPITE ADVANCED technology that can produce cars with 30 to 50 mpg and even much higher, many cars we drive today actually get fewer miles per gallon than cars did in the 1970s. The average fuel economy in the United States is a shockingly low 20.2 miles per gallon. (In Europe, that number is 35.) One reason for this poor average is that we're driving SUVs and big trucks, which average 18 mpg. Compare that to a 2007 Honda Civic, which gets 36 mpg on the highway and 25 mpg in the city. Or the Toyota Matrix wagon, which gets 33 mpg on the highway and 26 in the city.

SAVE
$884 or more every year by improving your fuel economy.

REDUCE
your car's yearly CO_2 output by 6,420 pounds.

Let's do the math. Say gasoline costs $2.75 per gallon and you drive 15,000 miles a year. **If your car gets 35 mpg, you'd spend $884 less on gasoline every year than if it got 20 mpg.** Invest that savings at an 8 percent rate of return and in 10 years you will have saved almost $14,000. In 20 years, you'll have almost $44,000, and in 30 years you'll have amassed more than $108,000!

Right now, decide to trade in your car for one with better fuel economy (higher mpg).

Have you heard about the "smart for-two" car from Europe that is being introduced in the United States? This hip and incredibly cute-looking two-seater, which is 8 feet 8 inches long and gets 40 mpg highway/33 city, promises to be a big seller when it hits the U.S. market in early 2008. The basic model starts at under $12,000. More than 30,000 people in the United States have already paid a $99 refundable deposit for their smart car. What are you waiting for? Check it out by visiting www.smartusa.com.

Upgrade to a Hybrid

A HYBRID CAR IS THE CLASSIC EXAMPLE OF WHY SOME people think that "going green" is a luxury they can't afford.

The Toyota Prius put hybrid cars on the map with a little help from Hollywood celebrities like Cameron Diaz. And hybrids do cost more than their nonhybrid counterparts. The 2008 Civic Hybrid, for instance, starts at $22,600, while the standard Civic starts at $15,010. So why should an ordinary person consider driving one?

SAVE
$1,147 per year.

SPARE
the environment 8,340 pounds of carbon dioxide.

First of all, a hybrid's engine runs on gas AND an electric battery that work together, so the car gets better gas mileage than even the most efficient gas-powered cars. The Honda Civic Hybrid gets 45 highway/ 40 city. The Toyota Prius gets an astounding 45 mpg highway/48 city.

But what about the sticker price? That's where the government comes in. By taking advantage of tax credits offered at the state and national levels, some buyers, according to the experts at Edmunds.com, recoup their investment in less than two years. And there is another way to cut the cost of a hybrid significantly—buy it used.

GO GREEN ACTION STEPS

☐ Find out if you can take advantage of a tax break. The Department of Energy's Fuel Economy web site has information on each hybrid model's tax breaks. Go to www.fueleconomy.gov and click on "Tax Incentives."

□ The credit amount (up to $3,000) depends on the number of individual cars sold for each model, and caps once the manufacturer sells 60,000 vehicles. So the Prius, for instance, is no longer eligible. (It's a shabby policy that needs to be amended. The government should be rewarding people for buying fuel-efficient cars—and manufacturers for producing them—not for buying the least popular models.)

□ Consider how much you drive. If you drive 15,000 miles per year, a hybrid that gets 45 mpg will use 417 less gallons of gas per year than a standard car at 20 mpg. That's a savings of $1,147 annually.

You might drive more or less. The more you drive, the faster you will get back your initial investment.

Go Biodiesel

MANY ORDINARY DIESEL CARS ALREADY GET BETTER gas mileage than their "regular" gasoline counterparts. But what makes diesel cars especially cool is that you can run them on biodiesel—a renewable fuel that's made from vegetable or animal fat, is nontoxic, and reduces greenhouse gas emissions by a phenomenal 75 percent. Any diesel car made since the mid-1990s can run on refined biodiesel (though you would need a modified engine to run it on waste vegetable oil). The catch is that, for the moment anyway, you can only use biodiesel fuel where you can find it.

Let's consider the benefit to your wallet. Standard diesel fuel currently costs about $3 a gallon, versus about $2.75 for regular gasoline. But a 2006 Volkswagen Jetta TDI gets 38 mpg on the highway—and some owners report getting upward of 50 mpg! If you drove 300 miles in the Jetta TDI, it would cost you about $21, while driving 300 miles in a 20 mpg "regular" gas car would cost you more than $40. And even though biodiesel costs slightly more than diesel, even at $3.20 a gallon that 300-mile trip would still cost an appealing $23.

SAVE
more than five cents for every mile you drive (or $800).

SAVE
750 gallons of gasoline.

GO GREEN ACTION STEPS

☐ Find out if you can buy biodiesel fuel in your area. Visit Biodiesel America at www. biodieselamerica. org to locate retail pumps, distributors, supplers—even co-ops, which let you buy the fuel at a lower price.

☐ Learn more about biodiesel initiatives in your area; join a forum and get your questions answered at www.biodieselnow. com.

GO GREEN
ACTION STEPS

☐ Get a tune-up.

☐ Buy a tire gauge. Tire gauges come in all shapes and sizes. Choose one that's easy for you to use (so you're more likely to use it). Visit: www.getagauge. com.

☐ Calculate your savings. The Department of Energy's Fuel Economy web site shows exactly how much you can save per gallon of gas just by keeping your car well maintained and by driving efficiently. Go to www.fuel economy.gov and click on "Gas Mileage Tips."

Maintenance Matters

NO MATTER WHAT CAR YOU DRIVE, MAINTAINING IT so that it's running at its highest efficiency is just common sense—the kind of sense that adds up to dollars.

- *Keep your tires properly inflated*. Having your tires inflated to the right pressure can increase your mpg by up to 3 percent, saving you up to 10 cents per gallon of fuel.
- *Don't haul around unnecessary weight*. What are you storing in your trunk? Unnecessary cargo weighs down your car and reduces your mpg.

SAVE *up to $798 in gas every year.*

KEEP *5,800 pounds of CO_2 out of the air each year.*

- *Get a tune-up.* Installing a clean air filter protects your engine and can increase your fuel economy by up to 10 percent, which translates to as much as 32 cents per gallon of gasoline.
- *Don't drive like a maniac.* Aggressive acceleration and braking can reduce your highway mileage by a third. Driving over 60 mph can cost you 20 cents per gallon of gas for every 5 mph increase.

☐ See how much you could save each and every month by giving up your car. Go to "The Real Cost of Car Ownership Calculator" at www.bikesatwork. com. or visit www. commutesolutions. com which lets you calculate your direct costs per mile as well as CO_2 emissions and land-use impact.

☐ For times when you do need a second car, could you sign up for a car-share program? ZipCar is a great option in 48 cities. Reserving a car for six two-hour slots and two four-hour slots each week costs only $162 a month. See if there's a ZipCar program in your city by going to www.zipcar. com. Or search other car-sharing programs at www. carsharing.net.

☐ Get out of your lease. Check out www.leasetrader. com to find out how to get out of your lease early.

Get Rid of a Car

THE FASTEST WAY I KNOW TO CUT EXPENSES IS TO GET RID of a family car. I know what you're thinking—***There's no way I could get rid of a car***—but just stop and think about it. My family went from two cars to none when we lived in Manhattan. Our friends thought we were crazy, even though New York has an excellent public transportation system. Factoring in car-repair expenses, insurance, parking, gas, and so on, we figure we saved nearly $80,000 during those five years.

Consider this: There are roughly two cars on the road for every household in the country. The average annual cost of just one of those cars—including gas, insurance, maintenance, registration, and depreciation—is $8,580. So do the math—***if your household income is $50,000 and you own two cars, you're working four months out of the year just to pay for them!***

If every family in the United States gave up one car, it would reduce the amount of carbon dioxide emitted by around 413 billion pounds a year. And that's not to mention the decrease in other types of pollutants from car exhaust, which can cause health problems like asthma and emphysema and generally make our air worse to breathe.

SAVE
$8,580 every year that you do without one car.

KEEP
3,640 pounds of carbon dioxide out of the air.

Skip a Trip

An astonishing 91 percent of Americans commute to work alone in their car, averaging 30 miles per round-trip. If every person in the United States cut out just one car commute per week by carpooling or taking public transportation, we'd reduce carbon emissions by 149 million tons.

My challenge to you is to find a way to replace just one weekly errand or one day's commute with an alternative form of transportation. This is not so daunting when you consider that *40 percent of all car trips we make in the United States are less than two miles*. That's a distance you could easily cover on a bicycle, even if you aren't in top physical condition.

SAVE

$215 a year.

If we all did, we'd **REDUCE** *carbon emissions by 149 million tons.*

As for other means of transportation, try using public transit or carpooling. If one driver in your household switched to public transit full-time, you'd reduce your household's carbon footprint by 30 percent. I walk a mile to work every day—burning my lunch off before I even eat it! Walking to work is free, and it saves you the cost of a gym membership.

GO GREEN ACTION STEPS

☐ Get a bike. Two great bikes for commuting are the Electra Amsterdam and the Trek Lime. The Amsterdam costs around $500 and comes with a headlight powered by your pedaling, a rack for carrying your briefcase,

In Copenhagen, Denmark, 36 percent of the population—about 600,000 people—bike to work and school every day on more than 200 miles of bike lanes.

and chain guards to keep your suit grease-free. Ask for one at your local bike shop, or find your nearest dealer at www.electrabike.com/home. The Lime, which costs about $600, has automatic shifting (much like a car) and a "seat trunk"—a compartment in the seat where you can stash your wallet, keys, and phone during the ride. Go to www.trekbikes.com/us/en and click on "Bike Path."

☐ Join Bicycle for a Day! Go to www.bicycleforaday.org, a charity founded by Matthew Modine to inspire people from all walks of life to join the worldwide movement to reduce global warming and carbon emissions caused by gas-powered vehicles.

☐ Connect with a carpool, or start one yourself, using one of these sites: www.erideshare.com

www.carpoolworld.com

GET ENERGY SMART

AFTER HOW WE DRIVE, THE NEXT-BEST OP-portunity for savings, of both money and greenhouse gas emissions, are the homes we live in. Our homes account for more than 20 percent of our national energy demand and produce more than 20 percent of our national carbon dioxide emissions. In fact, according to The Alliance to Save Energy, the average home emits twice as much CO_2 as the average car.

Why do our homes use so much energy? Two reasons: First, homes in this country have become "supersized." Back in 1973, a quarter of new houses were smaller than 1,200 square feet. Today, only 4 percent are. Between 1978 and 2006, the average home grew from 1,750 to nearly 2,500 square feet—more than a third larger. Now 23 percent of new homes in the United States are more than 3,000 square feet. And more space means more resources—to light, heat, and cool.

Second, all the stuff we buy to fill our homes and make them more comfortable—like big-screen TVs, computers, air conditioners, fancy kitchen applianc-es—simply devour amazing amounts of energy.

So the first thing I suggest to make your home greener and your wallet weightier is to consider downsizing—and consider it a lifestyle upgrade. You'll pocket the profits from selling the bigger house, and you'll reduce your monthly bills. If you're building new, build smaller. At a cost of $150 per square foot, for every 500 square feet you scale back, you'll save $75,000 on construction costs.

But on any scale, there are plenty of things you can do to get energy-smart and all-around green where you live. As I shared in the Introduction, one of the things that propelled me into living a greener lifestyle was moving into America's first environmentally advanced residential tower, the Solaire (www.thesolaire.com). It uses 35 percent less energy than a typical building of the same size and two-thirds as much water, and most of the materials used in building it have recycled content. A pesti-cide-free rooftop garden helps keep the apartments

warm in winter and cool in summer. And the building's developers selected materials and paints that have lower-than-normal emissions of toxic chemicals. As healthy as this building is for the planet, it's even healthier for the people living in it.

The most surprising thing to me about all this is that I am using *fewer* resources and spending *less* on energy, and yet I am actually getting *more* out of life. You might not live in a green building, but you can find many of the same benefits in the place you already live. Read on.

Get an Energy Audit

THE BEST PLACE TO START TO REDUCE YOUR HOME'S energy use and lower your utility bills is to get a professional home-energy audit. The results of an energy audit can lead you to make changes that will **save as much as 30 percent** on your utility bills. That is not small change when you consider that the cost to heat a home this year was almost $1,000.

Your first step is to call your local utility company and tell them you're interested in a whole-house evaluation. Many utility companies even offer this service for free to customers.

SAVE
up to 30 percent on your energy bills.

REDUCE
your CO_2 emissions by 9,515 pounds a year.

The audit should start with a review of your past utility bills, so be sure to have them handy. It will include a thorough room-by-room inspection of your heating/ cooling equipment, major appliances like your washer and dryer, lighting, and windows and doors. The energy expert who performs the audit will use certain tools and tests to evaluate your home. The blower door infiltration test will identify air leaks, and infrared cameras will reveal missing insulation, cold-air pathways, and moisture problems.

After the audit, you will be given a full report and a list of recommendations, including an estimate of how much the upgrades may cost and how much you can expect to save on future energy costs.

GO GREEN
ACTION STEPS

☐ Use the ENERGY STAR Home Energy Yardstick to compare your home's energy efficiency with that of similar homes across the country. You'll need your utility bills from the past 12 months, and once you answer a few questions about your home you'll receive a report of recommendations. Go to www.energystar.gov and click on "Home Improvements."

☐ To find a professional in your area who will conduct an energy audit, start with your local utility company. A state or local energy agency can also make a recommendation. You can even try the Yellow Pages under "Energy." Be sure to ask for references, and check them out with the Better Business Bureau by visiting www.BBB.org. A professional energy audit can cost $50 to $200—or even more, depending on where you live and how big your house is. But the investment is well worth it.

☐ If you prefer to start small, you can do a scaled-down energy audit yourself. Visit the Consumer's Guide to Energy Efficiency and Renewable Energy at www.eere.energy.gov. Just click on "Energy Audits" in the Quick Links section.

Run a Tight Ship

UNLESS YOU HAD YOUR HOUSE CUSTOM BUILT WITH energy efficiency in mind, chances are a home energy audit will reveal it's not as well sealed as it should be. Sealing leaks and adding insulation where needed are the cheapest and quickest energy improvements you can make to your home. In fact, according to the Environmental Protection Agency, fixing poor insulation and reducing drafts and other air leaks can save you up to 20 percent—several hundred dollars or more each year—on your utility bills, because you won't be paying to heat or cool air that then escapes from your house.

SAVE *up to 20 percent on your energy bills.*

REDUCE *your home's emissions of CO_2 by 2,808 pounds a year.*

Roughly half of our home energy expenses come from heating and cooling, which also sends 150 million tons of CO_2 emissions into the air every year.

You can easily fix leaks in attics, basements, crawl spaces and around doors, windows, and recessed lighting fixtures with inexpensive tools from your hardware store, like caulk and weather stripping.

Using tape or mastic to seal connections on heating ducts, then wrapping ducts in insulation can make your home's heating system 20 percent more efficient. It will also help keep out dust and toxins.

GO GREEN ACTION STEPS

☐ Download the *Guide to ENERGY STAR Home Sealing* at www.energystar.gov. Click on "Air Seal and Insulate" under Home Improvement. The site also offers tips on improving heating and cooling systems in your home. Click on "Heat and Cool Efficiently" under Home Improvement.

☐ Then download Xcel Energy's *Smart Energy Guide*, which offers detailed tips on reducing your home's energy loss. Find it at www.xcelenergy.com/docs/retail/SmartEnergyGuide.pdf.

☐ Seal leaks and add insulation where needed.

Get Green Energy

BRAD PITT IS LEADING A PROJECT IN NEW ORLEANS to build affordable homes that are completely powered by solar energy. "The idea that we pay utility bills is absolutely unnecessary," he says.

Is he right?

Today, 85 percent of energy in the United States comes from fossil fuels. They're called "fossil fuels" because they are the remains of organisms that lived roughly 300 million years ago. They include coal, oil, and gas, so chances are the home you live in is powered by one or more of these sources. There are two problems with that: One, they pollute our air and are the leading cause of global warming; and two,

they're nonrenewable resources, and many experts believe world production of oil could peak in the next two to twenty years.

So what can you (or even Brad Pitt) do about it? You have two options:

The first is to wait it out. Right now, your home is very likely connected to the "grid" of public utilities, which means you are dependent on whatever energy sources your local utilities provide. The exciting news is that the options are expanding.

For now, clean renewable energy is more expensive for utilities to access than fossil fuels. But as I write, massive amounts of money—close to $120 *billion* are

GO GREEN
ACTION STEPS

☐ Find out what type of green power is available to you right now, as well as what it costs, at the Department of Energy's Green Power Network. Go to www.eere. energy.gov/green power.

☐ Estimate the cost, size, and savings of a PV system, and find a solar energy professional in your area, at www. findsolar.com.

☐ To see what tax credits your state offers, visit the Database of State Incentives for Renewable Energy, www.dsireusa. org. The site also has information on the federal tax credit—just click on "Federal Incentives."

being invested in renewable-energy projects around the world. And much of that research is focused on creating *affordable* green energy sources.

Investment giant Goldman Sachs has already invested $1.5 billion in alternative energy and clean tech worldwide. Morgan Stanley estimates that global sales from clean-energy sources like wind, solar, geothermal power, and biofuels could grow to $1 trillion by 2030. Even Google's getting into the game! They recently announced plans to spend tens of millions of dollars on research and development and related investments in renewable energy. Their hope is that by funding research on promising technologies, investing in promising new companies, and doing a lot of their own R&D, they will help to "spark a green electricity revolution that will deliver breakthrough technologies priced lower than coal."

Go solar and one day...

PAY *ZERO for energy.*

REACH *ZERO emissions for the planet.*

Later in this book, you'll learn about how you, too, can invest in what promises to be a huge green economic boom. For now, it is enough to say that this massive investment is sure to transform the way your home is powered in the future. But what can you do right now?

Electricity from renewable sources might already be available to you. Call your utility company today to find out what your choices are right now. If there are no green choices available, you can probably opt to pay a small premium on your energy bill to support development of renewable energy. That's an investment you would make today to encourage availability of affordable sources in the future.

But there's a more aggressive choice you can make right now, and that is to install solar panels (photovoltaic panels, known as PV) on your home, helping to reduce your reliance on the utility grid. You don't have to be a movie star like Brad Pitt to let the star nearest to Earth power your home.

Converting to solar costs money, but tax incentives can slash the cost by as much as two-thirds, and once you've paid for the system, your electricity is free. A three-kilowatt system, which would generate most of the power for an average home, costs around $20,000 but may be reduced to as little as $7,000 by rebates and credits.

Think of financing a PV installation as paying a mortgage versus renting. Instead of sending money to the utility company every month (like rent), you're making payments on solar panels—an investment that not only saves you money over time but also increases the value of your home.

If a million homes went solar-powered, it would keep 4.3 million tons of CO_2 out of the air every year.

You can also go solar to meet your hot water needs, from sinks and showers to hot tubs to hot-water-heating systems. Solar thermal systems are less expensive to install than PV—roughly $3,500 to $5,000—and also qualify for tax credits and other incentives. Imagine having a home with zero utility costs! It's not just a dream. It's the new reality.

Do It by Degrees

WHEN I WAS A KID, I WOULD COMPLAIN THAT MY parents made us freeze in the winter. Turning the heat up would often cause a war, because Dad and Mom kept the thermostat at 67 degrees and told us to wear a sweater. Turns out my parents were "green" before green was in.

You don't have to freeze to be green. Adjusting your thermostat up or down by just three degrees Fahrenheit all year round will save you about $114 on a 1,500-square-foot home and will keep two and a half tons of carbon dioxide out of the atmosphere.

The biggest savings are seen during the colder months. For every degree you turn the heat down in winter, you'll bring your energy bill down by as much as 5 percent. According to the Department of Energy, lowering your thermostat by just one degree Fahrenheit— an imperceptible amount— can save up to $40 a year.

SAVE

$114 yearly on your energy bills.

REDUCE

your home's annual emissions of CO_2 by 2,683 pounds.

Melt 3 percent off your energy bill for every degree you turn the thermostat up in the summer.

If you install a programmable thermostat, that's even better. You can set it to turn your temperature way down or up when you're at work or sleeping. It'll cost you about $70, and it could save you $150 a year.

GO GREEN ACTION STEPS

☐ Learn how to install a programmable thermostat from actor/green guru Ed Begley in Home Depot's "Celebrity Workshops" series at www.homedepot clinics.com. Click on "Celebrity Workshops" in the online workshop section, then go to Begley's series and click on the thermostat video.

☐ Turn your thermostat down three degrees in winter, and program your thermostat way down at night and when you are at work or school.

GO GREEN ACTION STEPS

☐ Smart power strips can be purchased for about $35 apiece at any hardware store. Or shop online at the Smart Strip Store. Visit www.bitsltd.net.

☐ Switch the power strips off at night, when you are not home, when you are away, and when you are not using your appliances for an extended period.

Unplug It

IF THERE IS ONE OUTSTANDING EXAMPLE IN THIS book of stuff we spend money on for no good reason and *without even realizing it*, it is the energy drain known as "phantom load." Amazingly enough, even when your appliances are technically turned off, they continue to suck energy out of the wall and money out of your wallet. The phantom load accounts for more than 27 million tons of CO_2 emissions in the United States every year, as well as mountains of resources wasted to produce the power.

Your phantom load, also known as standby power or idle current, totals 5 to 15 percent of your monthly electricity bill. Cube-shaped transformers—those oversized AC plugs—have phantom loads of 20 to 50 percent of their regular energy use. They consume so much electricity that they're sometimes referred to as "vampires."

STRIP *$94 off your yearly electric bills.*

REDUCE *your home's emissions of CO_2 by 1,430 pounds per year.*

In all, Americans spend about $4 billion a year on electricity for things they're not using.

To eliminate phantom loads, you've got to unplug your devices and appliances. Make it easy on yourself by using smart power strips with on/off switches you can turn off when you're not running anything, when you go to sleep, and when you go away on vacation.

Be an ENERGY STAR

THIS ONE IS A NO-BRAINER. IT WILL SAVE A TON OF energy without much effort on your part at all, and save you a lot of money to boot.

ENERGY STAR has already helped us to collectively...

SAVE
enough energy to power 25 million cars.

SAVE
$14 billion on our utility bills.

By now you're probably familiar with the blue and white ENERGY STAR label, created by the Environmental Protection Agency (EPA) and the Department of Energy (DOE) to help consumers identify energy-efficient products. You can spot it on thousands of approved appliances and equipment in more than 50 categories for your home and office.

In 2006, Americans saved enough energy by using Energy Star appliances to avoid greenhouse gas emissions equivalent to those from 25 million cars—and also saved $14 billion on their utility bills.

That's a huge amount of savings, and it is only partly offset by the higher initial cost of these appliances. An ENERGY STAR washing machine, for example, costs about $150 over a less efficient model, but you'll save $50 a year on your energy bill. And it will cut water use by up to 7,000 gallons per year.

I wouldn't go out and replace a perfectly good (but inefficient) appliance for the $400 lifetime savings alone, but when it is time to buy a new one, make sure it has the ENERGY STAR label.

GO GREEN ACTION STEPS

☐ For info on Energy Star models, savings calculators, and energy efficiency tips, visit www.energystar.gov.

☐ For helpful tips on buying energy-saving appliances, check out the Natural Resources Defense Council web site. Visit www.nrdc.org and enter "appliances" in the search box.

☐ Some cities offer tax credits for installing energy-efficient appliances, which can save you even more money. Check with your utility company or local government office.

Think twice before breaking the bank to buy a plasma-screen high-definition TV. I admit I have one. But I didn't realize until I wrote this book that they can use nearly twice as much energy as their LCD-screen counterparts, and more than three times as much as the standard models. TVs account for 4 percent of our energy use nationally, and with more and more plasma models appearing in living rooms, that number could reach 8 percent before the decade is out.

Switch to Compact Fluorescent Bulbs

IN NOVEMBER 2006, WAL-MART, A COMPANY COM-mitted to "greening" its business, set a target of selling 100 million compact fluorescent bulbs (CFLs) before the end of 2007. The company reached its goal three months early, and as a result the bulbs Wal-Mart's customers bought will collectively save them $3 billion on energy costs and keep more than 22 million tons of greenhouse gases out of the atmosphere.

SAVE
$45 over the life-time of a bulb.

REDUCE
emissions of CO2 by 67 pounds over the lifetime of a bulb.

This, to me, is a prime example of how positive changes are being made in the "green space." Businesses like Wal-Mart are helping consumers like you to make easy choices that are better for your bottom line AND better for the planet. It is a huge win-win.

CFLs use *75 percent* less electricity than traditional incandescent bulbs and last up to *10 times longer*. They are more expensive—around $4 a bulb versus roughly $1—but the investment will pay for itself 10 times over during the life of the bulb. This is an easy one, folks.

GO GREEN ACTION STEPS

☐ As your existing bulbs burn out, replace them with CFLs.

☐ One drawback of CFLs is that they contain small amounts of mercury, so proper disposal will eventually be a concern. IKEA has stepped up to the plate by offering a CFL-recycling program (kudos to IKEA), and you can look for other local recycling options at www.earth911.org.

For 100 years, we've used "incandescent" bulbs to light our homes. They're incredibly inefficient; only about 5 percent of the energy supplied to them is converted into light. The newer technology, CFLs, are basically a bulb version of those tube-shaped fluorescent lights you're used to seeing—only softer and easier on the eyes.

Plant Trees

HERE'S AN INCREDIBLY SIMPLE WAY TO SAVE ON energy costs: Plant trees. Strategically planting trees and shrubs to shade your home can lower surrounding air temperatures during warm summer months by up to 9 degrees Fahrenheit—and can reduce your wall and roof temperatures by 20 to 40 degrees Fahrenheit, keeping your home naturally cooler.

In winter, trees can function as windbreaks as well, reducing your heating bill.

SAVE *$177 annually on energy costs.*

REDUCE *your home's emissions by 3,952 pounds per year.*

Over the course of a year, the average home could save between $150 and $250 on energy costs—simply with smart landscaping.

Of course, there are lots of other reasons to plant trees. Besides providing food and housing for insects, birds, and other backyard wildlife, trees protect against erosion and clean the air as they soak up carbon dioxide from the atmosphere. Just be sure to choose species that are either native to or well-suited for your location. You don't want your shade-bearer requiring excessive water or crowding out established elements of your garden.

GO GREEN ACTION STEPS

☐ Learn about landscape shading, including regional and microclimate considerations, at the Department of Energy's Energy Efficiency and Renewable

Energy site, www.
eere.energy.gov/
consumer. Click on
"Landscaping" in
the quick links.

☐ The National
Renewable Energy
Lab's guide *Land-
scaping for Energy
Efficiency* covers

the basics as well
as plant selection.
Download it at
www.nrel.gov. Type
"landscaping" into
the search box,
then click on the
name of the guide.

☐ Start plant-
ing practically
free. The Arbor
Day Foundation
offers ten free
shade trees when
you purchase an
annual member-
ship for $15. Their
site is an amazing

resource, with tons
of information on
planting, growing,
and learning about
trees. Visit them at
www.arborday.org.

GO LOW FLOW

WATER IS A GREAT EXAMPLE OF SOMETHING that is so cheap—less than a penny a gallon—that we take it for granted. We run the tap when we brush our teeth (at two gallons wasted per minute), we ignore leaks (5 to 10 percent of American homes are losing **_ninety gallons of water a day_** through leaks), and the result is that we end up spending $500 a year per household on something that is supposedly practically "free."

But it won't be free forever. As the Environmental Protection Agency points out, water is a finite resource. Even though 70 percent of the planet is covered by it, less than 1 percent is available for human use. The U.S. government predicts water shortages in 36 states between now and 2013. As I write this, there are serious drought conditions throughout the southern states, with Georgia actually experiencing a drought emergency.

The good news is it's possible to use up to 35 percent less water by making some fairly simple changes in our homes. Along with conserving this literally life-sustaining resource, you can save about $156 a year in the process.

☐ Start by fixing leaky pipes and fixtures—and don't forget sprinkler systems. The site www.h2ouse.org has some amazing resources, including instructions on how to use your water meter to detect unseen, silent leaks in your home.

☐ When you're replacing your toilet, buy a dual-flush model. Install low-flow showerheads now.

☐ For dozens of ways to save water, tailored to your region of the country, go to www.wateruseitwisely.com/100ways.

Turn Off the Tap

THERE ARE SO MANY WAYS TO SAVE WATER IN AND around your home, and some simply require a change of habit—like not running the tap while brushing your teeth and running the dishwasher only when it is full. ENERGY STAR appliances, discussed on page 44, are designed to be not only energy efficient but water efficient as well.

SAVE
$72 a year just in your bathroom.

CONSERVE
9,200 gallons of water per year.

Your toilet uses the most water of anything in your home. A regular toilet can use up to seven gallons of water every time you flush, depending on how old it is (new ones use 1.6). But the newer, dual-flush models have separate buttons for big and small flushes, using 1.6 and .9 gallons, respectively. They cost about $230 to $400, compared to about $175 for a standard model, but will save you 5,000 gallons of water a year. Install low-flow showerheads, too, and save 2,700 more.

Grow a Greener Lawn

FOR MANY HOMEOWNERS, A BEAUTIFUL LAWN IS important—it enhances the property, increases the home's value, and some may say that it even improves their quality of life. However, in most regions a lawn does not come naturally. ***Collectively, we use up to 7 billion gallons of water a day on landscape irrigation, a third of all residential water usage***. Up to half of that is wasted due to evaporation, wind, or overwatering. (Only an inch of water a week is necessary in many regions. Keep a cat-food-size can outside, and if rain fills it to the brim each week, you don't need to water at all.)

Some ways to reduce evaporation: Leave grass 3 to 4 inches long, water early in the morning, and leave some lawn clippings in place after mowing. Native plants require half the amount of water and help keep the local ecosystem in balance.

DECREASE your lawn's water use by up to half.

*We can all **SPARE** the environment 67 million pounds of chemicals each year by going organic in our yards.*

But wasting water might not be the worst thing we do with respect to our lawns. According to National Geographic's *The Green Guide* (www.thegreenguide.com), collectively Americans spend more than $38 billion each year—on chemical pesticides, insecticides, herbicides, and fungicides—to keep their lawns (all 30 million acres of them) looking great. A green lawn isn't really green at all. In fact, many of them are toxic.

If you're using these products or chemical fertilizers derived from fossil fuel (which adds to global warming), you're spending a lot of money to put the health of the planet, your family, and pets at risk. So what can you do about it? Go organic instead.

Pick up a do-it-yourself soil test kit at your local Lowe's or Home Depot. This will reveal what nutrients your lawn is lacking. Then feed your lawn with fertilizers, herbicides, and pesticides made from plant, animal, and mineral sources instead of those made from chemicals.

Gas-powered lawn mowers are also an environmental disaster—did you know they emit as much pollution in an hour as your car does traveling 100 miles? ***Mowers use 800 million gallons of gas each year, PLUS we spill a staggering 17 million gallons of gasoline a year while refueling them.*** (As a point of comparison, the 1989 *Exxon Valdez* tanker disaster in Alaska dumped 11 million gallons of oil.)

Trade in your gas mower for one that runs on electricity. They're quiet and clean and cost about $5 a year to run. Many manufacturers offer cordless electric mowers now. Better yet, get a push mower.

Your garden, too, could use an organic makeover. Compost, which is made of decomposed organic matter (things like food scraps, coffee grounds, and fallen leaves), is a great way to fortify the soil and keep your plants healthy—and cut down on the need for fertilizer and other chemicals. You can create compost in your own yard (even in your apartment), and doing so offers the added bonus of helping reduce the waste you send to landfills.

GO GREEN ACTION STEPS

☐ Stop wasting water on your lawn. Find more tips on water conservation on the web sites of most municipal water authorities, tailored to the needs of your region. The Pittsburgh Water and Sewer Authority web site, at www. pgh2o.com, is a good example.

☐ Do a soil test to see what nutrients

your lawn and garden need. Visit Lowe's Project and Video Center online at www.lowes.com for a how-to video on doing your own soil test.

☐ Help your lawn go organic. Visit www.thegreen guide.com and enter "lawn care" in the search box for a list of articles on nontoxic lawn care.

The *Wall Street Journal* recently ran a great article titled "Organic Lawn Care 101." You can find it at: www.realestate journal.com/ homegarden/ 20070712 -bounds. html.

For a whole library of how-to videos on organic gardens and to learn more about sustainable lawn care, visit www. safelawns.org.

There are many retail web sites that sell organic and eco-friendly lawn and garden products. Check out:

www.gardensalive. com

www.purebarn yard.com

www.extremely green.com

☐ Learn how and why to compost at www.compost guide.com.

Composting is relatively simple, but there are some rules to follow about what you can compost and how to maintain your pile.

☐ Go electric. Comparison-shop for an electric lawn mower at www. consumersearch. com and click on "Lawn Mowers" under "Lawn and Garden."

GREEN YOUR REAL
ESTATE STRATEGY

N THE FUTURE, GREEN WILL BE THE "NEW NORMAL."
Demand for green housing has already grown.
According to the National Association of Realtors,
46 percent of buyers would like a green home,
whereas only 2 percent of existing American homes
contain green features, according to a McGraw-Hill
Construction Information Group report released in
October 2007. Therefore, it makes no sense for you
to build a new house any other way.

Right now, a majority of Americans consistently
respond in surveys that they'll pay more for homes
that save energy, use recycled or sustainable materials, improve air quality, and save resources like old-
growth trees. Home values increase by roughly $20
for every $1 in annual energy savings, and green
materials can up the value even more.

Building a green home means setting higher
standards for energy efficiency and air quality, using sustainable or recycled materials, and keeping
waste to a minimum. And it's not necessarily more
expensive. According to What's Working (www.
whatsworking.com), a 15-year-old company that offers
training on green construction, a green home can be
built for less than 1 percent of additional cost when
compared to a traditional home. And you'll really
see the difference when you're ready to sell.

Granite countertops and cherry cabinets are yes-
terday's ideal. Tomorrow's buyers are going to want
low-VOC paint, recycled glass tiles, sunflower-based
panels (instead of plywood), and recycled marble
floors. And why shouldn't they? "Green" materials
look amazing, and as I said in this book's introduction, living in a green home has helped me feel better than I have in years.

If you're trying to sell right now and having
trouble, consider green upgrades that will let your
house "tell a green story" that makes it irresistible
to buyers.

Go Green, Live Rich

GO GREEN

50

*Simple Ways
to Save the
Earth and
Get Rich Trying*

LIVE RICH

David Bach
with Hillary Rosner

BROADWAY BOOKS
New York

PUBLISHED BY BROADWAY BOOKS

Published in the United States by Broadway Books, an imprint of The Doubleday Broadway Publishing Group, a division of Random House, Inc., New York. www.broadwaybooks.com.

BROADWAY BOOKS and its logo, a letter B bisected on the diagonal, are trademarks of Random House, Inc.

PHOTO CREDITS
Getty Images: pp. iv-v, 9, 11, 16, 19, 23, 30, 33, 37, 47, 49, 57, 58, 67, 85, 86, 95, 105, 109, 112, 115, 117, 127, 130, 133, 144, 147
© Corbis: pp. 25, 38-9, 53, 61, 63, 69, 77, 89, 91, 99
Veer: pp. 51, 97
Daimler Global Media: p. 21

BOOK DESIGN by Erin Mayes, EmDash

Cataloging-in-Publication Data is on file with the Library of Congress.

ISBN 978-0-7679-2973-8

PRINTED IN THE UNITED STATES OF AMERICA

10 9 8 7 6 5 4 3 2 1

First Edition

To my son Jack, I love you more than I ever knew it was possible to love.

*To my mom and dad,
now that I have a son I understand
how much you love me—
and how lucky I am for that love.*

Contents

Introduction

What if I told you that in just an hour or two I could share with you fifty simple tips that would have a dramatic impact on our ability to turn the tide on global warming, PLUS save you money and potentially turn you into a future "green millionaire"?

Most people fear global warming and want a healthier planet. I am sure you are one of these people or you would not be holding this book in your hands right now.

BUT most people also believe that "going green" is a luxury, an expensive choice they can't afford. What if I told you that going green doesn't have to be expensive—and, in fact, you can go green and SAVE money—and if you invest green you can get RICH?

What if there were easy, simple things you could do that not only protect the Earth but also protect your family's finances?

Would you spend a few hours with me to learn the ways? Would you join the movement to be "eco-friendlier" and environmentally conscious? Would you like to GO GREEN AND LIVE RICH?

—DAVID BACH

Saving the planet is the most important issue we face in our lifetime. This book looks different from any other book I have done because it *is* different. Please stop, turn to a page anywhere in the book right now, and see if "one green thing" grabs you. Then stop and ask yourself, *Why not me? Why not now?* Let's go green together.

Why Go Green?

You hold in your hands a book that could not only change your life but also help turn the tide on the devastating effect that global warming could have on our planet.

This is my ninth book in nine years, and it's very possible that you have read one or more of the previous eight. There are currently more than 5 million copies of my FinishRich Books in print. I'm known for my take-action advice on your finances. I've inspired and motivated millions around the world to be smarter with their money and to live and finish rich.

So why now write a book about "Going Green"—and why should you read it?

The answer is simple:

GOING GREEN IS THE MOST IMPORTANT ISSUE THAT WILL SHAPE OUR FUTURE.

I believe, as many around the world do, that we have reached a turning point (or tipping point, as Malcolm Gladwell would say) on the environment. We have come to a point in time where what we do as people to change the tide of global warming and reverse its effects on our planet requires stronger action than we have taken.

Second, I believe that the world IS taking action and that the United States in particular has lagged in its actions over the last twenty years and now needs to catch up. As citizens and tenants of our planet, we cannot allow the disaster of global warming to continue. We have to change the tide of the global warming epidemic, or our lives, our children's lives, and their children's lives will be forever affected.

We have done tremendous damage to our planet. We have been bad tenants, and the landlord (our planet) is suffering, but in truth it is we who will suffer the most if we don't do something and take drastic action.

Third, I am convinced that WE WILL TAKE ACTION, and that the action we take to become environmentally smarter will shape the environmental and economic futures of all of us.

GOING GREEN CAN MAKE YOU RICH—
NOT GOING GREEN CAN MAKE YOU POOR

I AM CONVINCED THAT WE ARE WAKING UP TO THE NEED TO LIVE GREENER and protect the planet. As a result one of the biggest factors affecting your ability to build wealth over the next twenty years is going to be the global environment and what we're doing (or not doing) to protect it.

If you missed investing in the computer and technology revolution in the 1980s and 1990s, you missed one of the biggest investment opportunities of the twentieth century. Well, green is the new technology. ***Investing green will be to the twenty-first century what investing in technology was to the twentieth century.*** From a financial point of view, you simply cannot afford to ignore it. This book will help you see the opportunities that exist to catch this life-changing movement.

GOING GREEN IS ABOUT OUR KIDS, OUR FAMILIES, OUR LIVES

AS I WRITE THIS, THE UNITED NATIONS FRAMEWORK CONVENTION ON Climate Change is meeting in Bali to set a global agenda for action. Earlier this year, the UN-sponsored Intergovernmental Panel on Climate Change (IPCC) completed its fourth assessment of the science and impacts of climate change. It concluded that greenhouse gas emissions from human activity rose by 70 percent from 1970 to 2004, and continue to rise at an increasing pace. As a result, climate change is "unequivocal." The impacts, according to the report, will include an increased risk of extreme-weather events such as hurricanes and drought, a decrease in the availability of fresh water for hundreds of millions of people, an increase in potentially deadly heat waves, and serious food-supply problems in Africa and other parts of the world. (I encourage you to read parts of this report at www.ipcc.ch. Look for "The AR4 Synthesis Report" and "Summary for Policymakers.")

As a father, I cannot read a report like this—supported by thousands of scientists and people from 130 countries—and not act. I cannot simply sit by knowing that one day I will have to explain to my son Jack why I didn't do anything to make a difference. And if you are a parent, I am sure you feel the same way.

As adults, we are not yet seeing the worst of the effects of global warming, but our kids, our grandchildren, and their kids will.

We must act and we must care. And we CAN do "something." Our kids who see our behavior change will change with us. In many cases, they are changing before we are. We may be learning now from them.

JUST DO ONE "GREEN THING TODAY"—IT WILL LEAD TO MORE

MY PERSONAL TRANSFORMATION TO BECOMING MORE ENVIRONMENTALLY conscious happened suddenly and, I must admit, by accident.

It started by doing "just one green thing." My green action was to move into one of the leading green apartment buildings in the country. I did this at the time not so much for the "green building" as for the location—the building was located next to my son's favorite park. But then something happened when I moved in and it stopped me in my tracks—our health improved within weeks.

For one thing, my allergies, which I had suffered from my entire life, simply disappeared. I was taking three prescription drugs a day when I moved in; within six weeks, I had pretty much stopped needing them. And my son's mild asthma disappeared completely. He has not had an asthma attack since we moved there (knock on wood). We have also started to sleep longer and more soundly.

I immediately started paying attention to the building. What was in this building and why were we feeling better? Why was it that a building that was designed to be environmentally friendly could make us feel better? Within weeks, I made more changes. My cleaning products at home are now all green. So are the dry cleaners we now use. I looked at my car, a gas-guzzling SUV, and gave it up. I also started noticing that I wasn't spending more money to make these changes. I was actually *saving* money! And then I started telling my friends (all of those who would listen).

Now, the truth is I'm still transforming, but I have become green-conscious—and it is changing both my life and that of my son.

I share this with you not to brag but to demonstrate that if a guy like me who used to hate to recycle can change, so can you. And that's what this book is meant to help you do—to take action to *Go Green and Live Rich!*

WHAT DOES IT MEAN TO LIVE RICH?

MANY OF THE BOOKS I'VE WRITTEN HAVE "FINISH RICH" IN THE TITLE. They have taught people with ordinary incomes, some of whom are living paycheck to paycheck, that they can afford to save for their future. One key step in that process is deciding to live in line with your values. For most families, a secure future IS a value, though not necessarily one that they are living.

Go Green, Live Rich is, like those books, about the kind of small daily savings that can add up to a richer future. But I decided to call it *Go Green, Live Rich* to make the point that living a life in line with your deepest values is a gift we give ourselves every single day. There is peace in knowing that the houses we live in, the way we work and travel, and our daily habits are serving the planet, our true home, not destroying it.

50 SIMPLE STEPS TO GO GREEN—PICK ONE TODAY

THE SURPRISING MESSAGE OF MY BOOK IS THAT YOU CAN HAVE IT BOTH ways. You can live a life in line with your green values AND you can put a million dollars in the bank. You can save the earth and get rich trying.

Go Green, Live Rich is organized into 50 "tips" of just two or three pages each, designed to make it easy for you to learn all you need to know about each "green thing." First, the chapter called "Know Your Impact" helps you understand the effects of your own current behavior on the planet in a way that I hope will motivate you to change. The next eight sections show you how to make greener choices in all the areas of your life, from driving the right car to making your home energy smart, from supporting green causes to making dinner for your kids. You will learn ways to spend less, save more, and pay fewer taxes, even as you are reducing your negative impact on the Earth. Each tip focuses on simple actions you can take, and I've provided all the resources—web sites, stores, and phone numbers—that you need to get started right away.

Then, once you've made a few changes, the section called "Finish RICH: Make Your First Green Million" will show you how to spin your green daily savings into gold.

BECOMING A GREEN MILLIONAIRE ON A FEW DOLLARS A DAY

SOME PEOPLE WILL READ THE TITLE OF THIS BOOK AND THINK, *GREEN IS FOR people who can afford to buy fancy organic coffee, not for me.* And if they flip through the book and look at some of the money-saving tips, they will say that saving 30 percent on their electric bill and 30 percent on their water bill, and even using hundreds of gallons less gasoline every year (which, as I write, costs nearly three dollars a gallon where I live), is nice but not enough to make a person rich. Well, they would be wrong.

THE LITTLE THINGS MAKE THE DIFFERENCE
BETWEEN RICH AND POOR

IF I HAVE LEARNED ONE THING IN MY NEARLY TWENTY YEARS AS A FINANCIAL advisor and coach, it is this:

It is not what you earn that makes you rich or poor; it is what you spend.

Millions of Americans are burning up money every day while they squander the planet's nonrenewable resources and pollute the environment in ways that lead to global warming and climate change. And we don't even realize it. *We are just doing things the way we have always done them.*

We buy a car because we like the way it looks and handles. We build a house with as many square feet as the bank's mortgage officer will allow. We renovate our kitchens with Sub-Zero refrigerators to increase our home's resale value. We run the sprinkler on our lawns using water that is so cheap that it is practically "free." It's all just common sense, right?

Wrong. There is a "new" way of doing all of these things that you will learn in this book. When you change your mind-set to a green way of thinking, you will change your actions, and those actions will put money back in your pocket. And over time, the money you save will make you rich.

Consider this: Perhaps, after you read this book, you will decide to try just four tips: 3, 10, 12, and 37. You improve your car's fuel economy and save $884 annually. You save $129 on your energy bills by sealing the leaks in your home, and $85 more by adjusting your thermostat three degrees. And you start bringing your lunch to work and pocket $1,560. That's a total of $3,758 per year, or approximately $10 a day of green savings.

And here's the best part: If you were to invest that $10 a day (instead of finding new things to spend it on), and you earn a 10 percent annual return (some of the green funds you'll learn about later have earned far higher returns), in 30 years you would have . . . $678,146.

With just four of the tips in this book you could earn nearly $700,000 for your future, all while living a greener lifestyle today. How many tips would you follow to become a Green Millionaire?

That is the promise of this little book. Imagine a present in which you are living lightly on the Earth, using power from renewable resources, breathing fresher air, and spending more time with the people you love. Then imagine that all the while you are building wealth—the kind of wealth that lets you do what you want to do when you want to do it, the kind of wealth that lets you give back so you can make a difference in the lives of others and in the fate of our planet. *That* is what it means to Go Green and Live Rich.

JOIN OUR COMMUNITY

My hope is that this book will inspire you to Go Green and Live Rich— and that you will prosper both personally and financially as a result. Will you let me know how it goes for you? You can email me your stories at success@greengreen.com. And please visit the new web site we have built at www.greengreen.com to help you live a greener life. I invite you to join our community there and get a free daily Green Tip of the Day.

However you get there, the journey to an environmentally friendly world is a journey we all need to take.

Live Green, Live Rich

David Bach

GETTING STARTED:
KNOW YOUR IMPACT

What can one person do to make a difference?

THE TRUTH IS, MANY OF OUR DAILY ACTIONS and behaviors add greenhouse gases to the atmosphere, and it's not entirely our fault. Many of the technologies, institutions, and ways of living that we embrace today were designed and created before we understood what the consequences would be.

But in December 2007 at the annual United Nations Framework Convention on Climate Change in Bali, 200 of the world's leading climate scientists issued a major call to arms. These scientists declared that we have only a small window of time in which to reduce worldwide greenhouse gas emissions in order to prevent some of the drastic impacts of global warming.

In the next 10 to 15 years, they said, emissions must begin to decline each year rather than grow—and by 2050, emissions must be *half* what they were in 1990. If we don't accomplish this, the scientists wrote, *many millions of people will be at risk from extreme events such as heat waves, drought, floods and storms, our coasts and cities will be threatened by rising sea levels, and many ecosystems, plants and animal species will be in serious danger of extinction.*

That's a lot to digest. But rather than being overwhelmed, let's start with what you can do today. One person can make a huge difference. Making changes in the way in which we live is key not only to our health and happiness—but to our survival as well.

Not too long ago, I decided to figure out just how much I personally was contributing to global warming by calculating my carbon footprint. The measure of our impact is often called a carbon footprint because carbon dioxide is the most common greenhouse gas.

Considering that I live in an eco-friendly apartment building, recycle, walk to work, and no longer own a car, I assumed my impact on the planet would be relatively low. It turns out that because I fly so often, my carbon footprint is much higher than I

thought. Doing this one simple exercise quickly
showed me changes I could make to lower my carbon footprint and inspired me to do more.

Now it's your turn. As your first step on the journey to going green and living rich, turn the page
and learn how to "know your impact."

Calculate your carbon footprint

CALCULATING YOUR CARBON FOOTPRINT—USING simple online tools that take about 3 minutes—is one of the easiest things you can do now to start going green. It will help you gain an understanding of just how your own actions and lifestyle actually impact this planet. Like me, you might be quite surprised by your results.

One of the best carbon footprint calculators is the one powered by EarthLab, an online "climate crisis community," which can be found at www.earthlab.com/carbonprofile.

Take a few moments to calculate your carbon footprint right now. The calculators will ask you to consider factors like where you live, how you work, and how you commute and travel—all things that *Go Green, Live Rich* will show you new ways to do.

How did you do? Once you have your score, the next step is to lower it. I know you can do better, and so can I. Read on.

GO GREEN ACTION STEPS

☐ Calculate your carbon footprint at www.earthlab.com/carbonprofile. Here are some others you can check out as well: www.fightglobalwarming.com/carboncalculator.cfm

www.epa.gov/climatechange/emissions/ind_calculator.html

www.zerofootprintoffsets.com

☐ Make up your mind to lower your score.

Find your Litter Factor

MAYBE YOU HAVE HEARD OF "THE LATTE FACTOR.®" It is a phrase I created as a metaphor for all the little things we spend money on over the course of a day without giving it much thought. The phrase applies to buying not only fancy coffee but also fast food, cigarettes, bottled water—you name it. I have long encouraged my readers to identify their "Latte Factor" and eliminate it to start saving money. But small changes such as not buying coffee in a disposable cup or water in a plastic bottle not only are good for your wallet, they actually better the planet. In the same way that "little things" add up to drain your wealth, "small changes" add up to make a big difference for the Earth.

SAVE

$500 in a year by breaking a bottle-a-day water habit.

RUN

100,000 cars each year on the oil saved if bottled water were history.

Consider this: **Every year, Americans drink more than 100 billion cups of coffee. Of these, 14.4 billion are served in disposable paper cups, enough to wrap the Earth 55 times if placed end to end!** Plus, those paper cups contain a plastic lining made from a petrochemical that would produce enough energy to heat 8,300 homes for a year.

Or this: A 2007 article by Charles Fishman in *Fast Company* magazine reports that North Americans spent $15 billion on bottled water in 2006. Fishman points out that transporting this water requires moving 1 billion bottles of water around *per week* in ships, trains, and trucks across the United States.

Not only that, but you could run 100,000 cars for a year on the amount of oil required to make the plastic used for bottled water. What's more, nearly 9 out of 10 plastic water bottles are simply thrown away, filling our landfills and blowing into our waterways. That's because 96 percent of the bottles sold in 2005 were single-serving sizes, which have a lower recycling rate than nearly any other type of plastic packaging.

That is how your Latte Factor—in this case, your Designer Water Factor—becomes your Litter Factor. I put this tip right up in the front of the book because it is a perfect example of how **wasting money and hurting the planet go hand in hand.**

And here's the truly crazy part—we drink designer water because we think it's healthier than "free" water from our taps. In reality, according to Fishman's article, 24 percent of the bottled water we drink (nearly one in four bottles) is tap water repackaged by Coke and Pepsi. Pepsi's brand is Aquafina—again, just purified tap water—and it costs nearly 2,500 times more than what comes out of your faucet. To drink the recommended amount of water (8 to 12 cups a day), you'd spend about $2,500 a year on Aquafina. The cost for the same amount of tap water? A dollar.

If you're buying actual spring water, like Evian, Poland Spring, or FIJI, chances are you're spending

GO GREEN ACTION STEPS

☐ See how it all adds up. Calculate your savings from breaking the bottled water habit by using my Latte Factor calculator at www.finishrich.com. Click on the "Learn" tab and select "Find Your Latte Factor."

Build Green (Buy or Rent Green, Too)

GENERALLY SPEAKING, THE GREENEST REAL ESTATE option is using what you've got, so consider remodeling instead of building new. If you intend to build green, start with the U.S. Green Building Council's *Green Home Guide* (www.greenhomeguide.org). You'll find definitions, resources, and inspiration for building or remodeling a green home.

INCREASE
your home's resale value by building green.

SAVE
a clear-cut acre of trees by using less wood or alternative materials.

It is important to consider materials. Sixty percent of all the trees we log domestically are used to build houses, and the average new 2,000-square-foot home requires an entire clear-cut acre's worth of wood (several hundred to several thousand trees). The typical home also uses nearly 17 tons of concrete, which contains cement—a material responsible for 5 percent of all greenhouse gas emissions worldwide.

Use wood that's sustainably grown, or consider alternatives to wood, such as straw bales or structural panels made of recycled polystyrene. Before you

buy bamboo, a popular new material, ask whether the bamboo has been treated with formaldehyde and if it comes from a truly sustainable source. For flooring, consider cork—which is sustainable and durable—as an alternative.

Skip vinyl. Twice as many homeowners choose vinyl siding as any other material—despite the fact that the production of vinyl is incredibly toxic.

Finally, to improve indoor air quality, use low-VOC paint, which cuts down on "volatile organic compounds," ingredients that can cause health problems, including cancer.

GO GREEN
ACTION STEPS

☐ Get the U.S. Green Building Council's *Green Home Guide* at www.greenhome guide.org. The USGBC also runs the LEED (Leadership in Energy and Environmental Design) certification program, which is a voluntary rating system for green buildings.

☐ Browse listings for green architects and builders at sustainable-design company Vivavi's *Modern Green Living Home Directory,* http://www.modern greenliving.com.

If you'd rather buy green or if you are renting, Vivavi also lists realtors.

☐ Choose greener materials.

☐ Visit your local used building materials yard for all sorts of interesting materials, from structural elements to windows and doors to design features like siding from an old barn or floors from a school gym. For resources that will help you find used building materials, visit www. buildingreuse. org/directory. The

nonprofit Habit for Humanity operates a series of retail material reuse stores called ReStores. For a directory, visit www. habitat.org and enter "ReStores" in the search box.

☐ Find out if you qualify for an EEM. Check the eligibility requirements at the Department of Housing and Urban Development's web site. Go to www.hud.gov/ offices/hsg; click on "Single Family" and then on "FHA Insured Loans" and then on "Energy-Efficient Mortgage Program."

For more information on EEMs, and how they can increase your borrowing power, read the Federal Citizen Information Center's Energy Efficient Mortgage Home Owner Guide. Go to www. resnet.us, scroll down to "Related Sites," and click on "HERS/EEMS." Then click on the name of the guide.

☐ Ask your lender if they offer energy-related incentives. Bank of America recently launched their "Energy Credit Mortgage Program," which offers $1,000 back on closing fees for new homes that meet ENERGY STAR requirements.

Get a Green Mortgage

LUCKILY, THE GOVERNMENT WANTS TO HELP YOU build green. Energy Efficient Mortgages (EEMs) are available as part of a federal program to help homebuyers finance energy efficiency upgrades and purchase energy-efficient homes. With an EEM, you can take out a bigger loan in order to buy a greener home—or you can use the money in the form of a home equity line of credit (HELOC) to pay for improvements to the efficiency of your existing home.

SAVE
$1,000 on closing costs.

INCREASE
your home's value by 5 percent.

The idea is simple. An energy-efficient home costs less to operate. With cheaper utility bills, the bank knows you'll be able to afford a larger mortgage.

New homes are eligible for these mortgages if the builder certifies that the home meets certain guidelines required by the lender. For existing homes, you'll need a home energy rating system report (HERS), which costs between $100 and $300. The report will rate the home on an index scale, then suggest improvements and costs. But your improvements will add value to your home. According to Energy Star, a HERS certification showing that a home is energy efficient can increase its value by roughly 5 percent.

SHOP GREEN,
SPEND *LESS*

BY NOW I HOPE YOU'VE LEARNED THAT GOING green does not have to be more costly and can, in fact, save you hundreds of dollars on your home's overhead expenses. But you might be thinking that the savings stop at your door. Doesn't it still cost more to buy green products at the grocery store—and, for that matter, at any other kind of store?

The short answer is no. And here's why: ***Your spending choices shape the world we live in.*** How you spend not only determines the quality of your life—what you eat, where you live—it also contributes to the success of the businesses where you shop. And as more and more Americans are choosing greener products, the prices are dropping all the time. That just makes sense, right?

For example, as ordinary Americans have become conscious of shopping for food grown without chemical pesticides, supermarkets have begun marketing store brands of low-priced organic foods. Safeway introduced its O brand, an organic line that includes 150 products across the store, from bread to olive oil to yogurt. And Whole Foods has a popular brand called 365, which includes competitively priced organic and all-natural products.

Not only are these products cheaper than name-brand organics, they're also often cheaper than the non-organic alternative. A 15-ounce can of O organic black beans costs $1.05. Whole Foods' 365 label organic beans are 99 cents. Compare that to a can of Bush's Best beans, on the shelf at Safeway for $1.39.

A bag of O pasta costs $1.95—just slightly more than a box of Barilla brand pasta, which sells for $1.79. But a bag of Whole Foods' 365 organic pasta costs $1.29—a savings of 50 cents a bag!

If we all begin to shop green and demand environmentally friendly products and services, the companies of the world will keep delivering them at more and more affordable prices. I believe it won't be very long before the cost of green products reaches parity with non-green products, and not much longer after that before the green alternatives become even cheaper.

In the meantime, shopping green does not have to mean paying premium prices. Even with categories that are still significantly more expensive, like organic produce, there are ways you can come out ahead at the grocery store. So let's go shopping.

GO GREEN
ACTION STEPS

☐ Join a bulk-buying club or cooperative where you can purchase larger-sized containers of almost anything you use in your home. Costco (www.costco.com) and Sam's Club (www.samsclub.com) are two great options.

Buy in Bulk

BUYING IN BULK DOESN'T MEAN PURCHASING LARGE cases of individually wrapped goods, and it certainly doesn't mean buying things you don't really need because you couldn't resist the bargain. Buying in bulk DOES mean buying the largest size of a product that you were going to purchase anyway. A 64-ounce bottle of laundry detergent is better for the planet than the 32-ounce bottle because it uses the smallest amount of packaging *per unit*—in this case, per ounce.

SAVE
up to a third on many groceries.

REDUCE
the 80 million tons of packaging that enters landfills each year.

Containers and packaging make up more than 31 percent of all municipal solid waste—almost 80 million tons in 2006. Think how much less waste there would be in landfills if we all bought in bulk whenever we could. And it is better for your shopping bill, because the larger size almost always costs less per pill, per drop of shampoo, per flake of cereal, and so on.

The bulk-bin aisle at your supermarket is another way to save. You can dispense dry goods like pasta, rice, cereal, nuts, dried fruit, and spices into your own bags, at much lower prices per unit. Some stores also sell bulk liquids this way, like cooking oil, soap, shampoo, and lotion.

☐ Find a super-market where you can buy natural foods in big bins. Whole Foods, which has 265 stores as of this writing, has a large selection of bulk bins. So will your local health food store or natural foods market.

☐ If you don't have options for buying organic in your area, consider forming a co-op with friends or neighbors, which enables you to place bulk orders at wholesale prices. Learn more at www.vegfamily. com by searching on "co-op food buying."

Planet-friendly beauty company

Aveda says its liter bottles contain 40 percent less plastic and cost 30 percent less than the equivalent amount in smaller bottles. A 15-ounce bag of organic beans from Shiloh Farms costs $2.69, but the company also sells a 25-pound bag that costs $1.69 per pound—a savings of more than a third.

Bring Your Bags

PAPER OR PLASTIC? THE BEST ANSWER FOR THE planet is *No, thank you.*

One of the easiest things you can do to save the Earth and get rich trying is bring your own bags to the grocery store. Many stores now offer "bag credits," discounts of between 5 and 10 cents a bag if you bring your own. Buy six bags of groceries a week and save up to $31 a year. The positive impact of skipping plastic bags is huge. Between 500 billion and a trillion plastic bags are used every year worldwide. As many as 30 billion of them end up as litter—making their way into our oceans, killing birds, marine mammals, and sea creatures by the millions.

SAVE
$31 a year at the checkout.

REDUCE
the 30 billion plastic bags that end up as litter each year worldwide.

That's because man-made plastics *photodegrade*, which means that sunlight breaks them down into smaller pieces—often tiny pieces, perfect for wildlife to mistake for food. And they don't *biodegrade*, meaning they stick around for thousands of years.

But believe it or not, paper bags may be worse. According to the Institute for Lifecycle Environmental Assessment (www.ilea.org), even though Americans recycled nearly 20 percent of paper bags (compared with less than 1 percent of plastic), one paper bag takes more energy to make and creates more waste than two plastic bags.

GO GREEN ACTION STEPS

☐ Bring your own bags to the store when you shop. Visit www.reusablebags.com for facts on reusable bags and other eco-friendly packaging, plus a store that offers reusable bags and water bottles that make great gifts.

Following the lead of countries that ban or heavily tax the use of plastic bags, including Ireland, Australia, and South Africa, forward-thinking U.S. cities have begun taking a stand. San Francisco banned them in March 2007. New Haven, Annapolis, Santa Monica, and New York City are all considering similar legislation. Read about plastic bag bans, including San Francisco's, at www.treehugger.com. Search "plastic bag ban."

GO GREEN
ACTION STEPS

☐ Go vegetarian
one extra day a
week. There are
thousands of easy-
to-prepare, tasty,
meat-free recipes
on the web. Start
at www.vegweb.
com.

☐ Find more
recipes, plus
read more about
meat's impact on
the environment,
at www.goveg.com
under "Environ-
ment." Click on
"Recipes" for
menus, nutrition
information, and
tips on eating
meat-free.

Eat Less Meat

MY MOST RECENT PHYSICAL SHOWED SUCH HIGH
cholesterol that my doctor wanted to put me on
medication. My response was "First let me see what
I can do to change my diet."

You probably already know that eating less meat
is better for your health—but did you know that it's
better on the environment, too?

Here are some facts that blew me away: Methane from captive livestock accounts for nearly a
fifth of all greenhouse gas emissions caused by
humans. In fact, a 2006 study called "Diet, Energy and Global Warming," by two University of
Chicago geophysicists, con-
cluded that switching from a
"Standard American Diet" to
a vegetarian diet takes a bigger bite out of global warming than trading in your SUV
for a hybrid car!

Eating less meat will also
result in savings for you. A
pound of ground beef costs
about $3.50, whereas a pound
of organic lentils costs about $2—and will yield
around 13 servings, packed with nearly as much
protein as the beef.

So give it a try. You don't have to become a vegetarian. Just try cutting out meat one day a week to
start with.

SAVE

*at least $6 on your
weekly grocery bill.*

REDUCE

*the 1.4 billion tons
of animal waste
generated by
U.S. factory farms
each year.*

There are other environmental costs from growing meat. The vast tracts of Amazon rain forest that have been cleared in recent decades are used mainly for beef production, either for grazing cattle or for growing soy to feed them. Plus, producing a pound of beef requires 30 times more water than producing a pound of wheat, and 200 times more than a pound of potatoes. Producing one calorie of animal protein uses 10 times as much fossil fuel as producing a calorie of vegetable protein. And the Environmental Protection Agency reports that animal waste from U.S. factory farms pollutes American waterways more than all other industrial sources combined. To learn more, read "The Case Against Meat," an article in *E/The Environmental Magazine,* at www.emagazine.com.

Grow Your Own

I ONCE SAW A BUMPER STICKER ON THE BACK OF A truck: "If you bought it, a truck brought it." Our food travels an average of 1,500 to 2,500 miles to reach our plates. That's a lot of gas and fumes—not to mention fossil fuels for pesticides, tractors, processing, cool storage, and packaging.

Instead, grow your own fruits and vegetables and reap the rewards. You'll save money, you'll know exactly how your food was grown and what went into it, and you'll connect with nature in a way that comes only from planting a seed and watching it grow up into a head of broccoli or a lemon tree.

SAVE
on produce by growing your own.

REDUCE
the miles traveled by your food to your plate.

A pack of tomato seeds costs about $3—about the same as a pound of tomatoes at the supermarket. But the seeds will produce enough fresh, tasty tomatoes to last you all summer long.

If you can't grow your own, your local farmer's market may still be a better choice than the grocery store to save on "food miles."

GO GREEN ACTION STEPS

☐ Get started on a vegetable garden. Learn everything you need to know about planting at www.backyardgardener.com/veg or www.thegardenhelper.com/vegetables.html. Buy organic seeds and garden supplies, plus find gardening information, at www.seedsofchange.com.

☐ If you are an apartment dweller, check out a long list of plants that thrive in pots (known as "container gardening") at www.containergardeningtips.com.

☐ Find a farmer's market near you, or locate other locally grown sources of food, at Local Harvest, www.localharvest.org.

For a telling look at the miles traveled by various foods, read "How Far Do Your Fruits and Vegetables Travel?" You can find it at the Leopold Center for Sustainable Agriculture's web site, www.leopold.iastate.edu. Scroll down to "Publications" on the left-hand side and click on "Other Publications."

Use Recycled Paper Products

THE PAPER PRODUCTS THAT WE USE EVERY DAY IN our homes—like toilet paper, tissue, paper towels, and napkins—are made from what's called virgin tree fibers. Consumers tend to prefer virgin fiber for its softness. But virgin fiber comes from old-growth trees, and entire forests of them are clear-cut in order to produce it. As more forests are destroyed, we have fewer trees to help keep our soil and water clean, provide habitat for wildlife, and soak up the carbon dioxide that causes global warming.

You **SAVE** *$39.53 annually by switching to recycled toilet paper.*

We could **ALL SAVE** *19 million trees.*

Consider what would happen if you switched to recycled toilet paper, tissue, paper towels, and napkins. According to Seventh Generation(www.seventhgeneration.com), if every household in the United States replaced just one four-pack of 400-sheet virgin fiber toilet paper with 100 percent recycled ones, we could save:

- 1,450,000 trees
- 3.7 million cubic feet of landfill space, equal to 5,500 full garbage trucks
- 523 million gallons of water, a year's supply for 4,100 families of four, and avoid 89,000 pounds of pollution!

And, what's more, Seventh Generation's recycled-fiber toilet paper costs less per square foot than most of the leading brands—reason enough to make the switch.

GO GREEN ACTION STEPS

☐ Buy recycled toilet paper and other paper products. Learn which brands to buy or avoid at www.nrdc.org/greenliving. Click on "Tissue Paper Guide for Consumers."

The Natural Resources Defense Council rates paper products based on recycled content and whether they are chlorine-free. Chlorine, a whitener, releases toxins into our air and water when combined with other chemicals.

Clean Green

THE AVERAGE U.S. HOUSEHOLD SHELLS OUT ROUGH-
ly $600 a year on 40 pounds of chemical cleaning
supplies. Yet for about $20, you can replace every
cleaning product in your house with a safer, nontoxic, biodegradable homemade version using common ingredients like baking soda, club soda, vin-
egar, and salt.

It is a huge irony that the products we buy to
keep our homes clean are a source of poisonous
chemicals—toxins that cause
cancer, asthma, and other lung
problems. Chemical cleaning
supplies are an $18 billion
industry, and they not only
threaten our health, they also
end up in our rivers, oceans,
soil, and air.

SAVE

*$580 a year by
making your own
nontoxic cleaning
products.*

SPARE

*the environment
40 pounds of toxic
chemicals.*

If you're not up for making
your own, there are nontoxic
commercial alternatives as well.
Two of my favorite brands—Shaklee and Seventh
Generation—offer cleaning products made with
safe, biodegradable ingredients at prices comparable to those of the mainstream brands.

GO GREEN ACTION STEPS

☐ **Buy nontoxic
cleaners.** Visit
www.Shaklee.com
and take a look at
"The Get Clean™
Starter Kit." You
can't buy Shaklee
in stores—only on
their web site or
through indepen-
dent distributors
listed on their web
site. Other green
brands, like those
made by Seventh
Generation (down-
load a coupon

at www.seventh generation.com), can be found at all natural food markets as well as many supermarkets. Some other brands to look for:

● **Ecover:** www. ecover.com

● **Earth Friendly Products:** www.ecos.com

● **Mrs. Meyer's Clean Day:** www. mrsmeyers.com

☐ Make your own inexpensive homemade cleaning products. You'll find recipes at www.greenpeace. org/usa. Just type "household cleaner recipes" into the search box.

More great recipes are at www. eartheasy.com. Click on "Live" and then on "Non-Toxic Home Cleaning."

☐ For help deciphering labels, and to learn what to look for to ensure you're not buying harmful cleaners, visit the Eco-Labels Center at Consumer Reports Greener Choices. Go to www. greenerchoices. org/eco-labels and click on "Household Cleaners."

☐ Don't spill your existing products down the drain. Find out how to properly dispose of these products in your area at www. earth911.org.

The Beauty of Going Green

HERE'S A CHALLENGE. GO INTO YOUR BATHROOM right now and count all the bottles and jars of half-used hair gels, moisturizers, antiperspirants, and makeup that you've abandoned because some newer product caught your eye. The average U.S. household spends about $600 a year on personal-care products, many of which we never use up.

It turns out that many of these products contain ingredients that are bad for us and potentially worse for the planet.

Many standard ingredients in your daily beauty routine are made from petroleum, and many are potential carcinogens or hormone disrupters, which when they're washed down drains and into streams and rivers can have serious impacts on wildlife—causing fish to change sex, for instance. In 2002, the first national study of hormone disrupters and other man-made chemicals in our waterways found that 80 percent of the streams tested were contaminated.

There are plenty of products—we've listed many brands on the next page—that you can buy that contain natural, planet-friendly ingredients, smell great, aren't tested on animals, and don't cost any more than the chemical-filled varieties.

☐ Find a simple, healthy beauty routine and stick to it. Look for companies whose sustainable practices extend to their packaging, energy use, and store design. You can start with the list on the facing page.

At Environmental Working Group (www.ewg.org), learn about toxic chemicals that might be hiding in your personal-care products. Click on "Chemical Index" to look up specific ingredients and their health effects. Or click on "Health/Toxics" for news and in-depth research into the ingredients in cosmetics and other products.

- **Alba Botanica** (www.albabotanica.com)

- **Avalon Organics** (www.avalonorganics.com)

- **Aveda** (www.aveda.com)

- **Burt's Bees** (www.burtsbees.com)

- **Desert Essence** (www.desertessence.com)

- **EO Products** (www.eoproducts.com)

- **Kiss My Face** (www.kissmyface.com)

- **Nature's Gate** (www.natures-gate.com)

- **Origins** (www.origins.com)

- **Recycline** (www.recycline.com)

- **Simply Soaps** (www.simplysoaps.com)

- **The Organic Pharmacy** (www.theorganicpharmacy.com)

- **Tom's of Maine** (www.tomsofmaine.com)

You can buy these brands at health food stores, at natural foods supermarkets like Whole Foods and Wild Oats, at some regular supermarkets and drugstores, and at sustainably minded pharmacies like Pharmaca (www.pharmaca.com)—a growing chain based in Colorado and with stores in several cities around the West.

Green Your Decor

"GREEN" FURNITURE IS A GREAT EXAMPLE OF A PRODuct whose prices are coming down as more and more companies manufacture furniture from sustainable, safe materials. At Viva Terra, you can buy a bookcase made of sustainably harvested wood for $679, a savings of more than $400 over Pottery Barn's comparable bookcase built from medium-density fiberboard and containing formaldehyde and lacquer. Which would you rather have in your home?

SAVE
*up to $400 on a
major purchase.*

GREENGUARD
*has certified
150,000 low-emission products for
indoor use.*

We spend about $78 billion a year on new furniture in the United States, and much of what is on the market today contains PBDEs (legally required flame retardants that cause health problems) and/or finishes and lacquers that release volatile organic compounds (which can cause lung damage), formaldehyde and benzidine (which can cause cancer), and many other harmful chemicals.

This is a case where we must use our spending choices to create the kind of world—and living rooms—we want to live in. Seek out sustainable items—that means items made from responsibly harvested, renewable, or reclaimed materials that contain little or no toxic chemicals. They're better for the environment and for your health.

**GO GREEN
ACTION STEPS**

☐ Shop online
for sustainable
furniture at

www.vivaterra.com

www.greenerlife
styles.com

www.pristine
planet.com

www.eyezotica.com

www.ecobedroom.
com

☐ Look for products certified by GreenGuard, an independent certification system for products with low levels of toxic emissions. Go to www.greenguard. org.

☐ Look for the seal of approval from the Forest Stewardship Council (FSC), which certifies lumber cut in an environmentally responsible manner. Learn more at www.fscus.org.

PROFIT BY
RECYCLING

7

WE LIVE IN A THROW-AWAY SOCIETY. You'd be amazed at what some people throw away—everything from bathtubs to books. But the truth is, there's no such place as "away." Every day in the United States, roughly 690,000 tons of materials are dumped in landfills, according to the Environmental Protection Agency. And only a small fraction of that is legitimate waste.

If you've read my book *Start Late, Finish Rich*, then you are familiar with my advice to people who want to earn money on the side. In the book, I wrote about how to get rich on eBay, and it turns out that this is also excellent advice for people who want to go green AND make more money.

It sounds absurd, but you CAN profit by recycling. By selling the things that you are accustomed to throwing away. By buying used. By not buying just because there's a newer model. It's a whole new way of thinking about your "stuff." Some communities are even offering cash incentives for people who require less trash pickup, which you almost certainly will if you are dedicated to reusing, reselling, recycling, and gifting the things you no longer need. Read on to learn how.

Buy and Sell Everything

EVEN THOUGH *YOU* MAY NO LONGER WANT YOUR old rug or toaster, someone else will.

In New York, moving often means putting the "junk" you no longer want out on the curb and coming back half an hour later to find that it is gone. Clearly, your trash is someone else's treasure. And they might be willing to pay for it, too. As evidence, people traded *$52 **billion worth*** of items last year on eBay. That is $210 per user. Craigslist.org is another great place to sell your stuff, and because it's local it keeps shipping (which requires packaging and fuel) to a minimum.

Think before you buy, too. Do you really need an upgrade to replace something that works perfectly well? Buy used whenever possible. Why pay $250 or more for a brand-new futon frame, for instance, when you might find a barely used one for free on Freecycle.com? This is the kind of "green thinking" that puts money in your pocket by helping you not to take out your wallet in the first place.

MAKE *$210 this year—or a lot more—selling your unwanted stuff on eBay.*

We can **ALL SAVE** *300 tons a day— or a lot more— from going into landfills.*

GO GREEN ACTION STEPS

☐ Set up an eBay account and start selling your unwanted stuff for a profit. Visit www. ebay.com.

☐ Look for bargains online. Craigslist offers online classifieds for 450 cities worldwide. To find the listings for your area, go to www.craigslist.org.

☐ Shop for free. The Freecycle Network has more than 4 million members in 75 countries. It's a grassroots, nonprofit movement of people who are giving (and getting) stuff for free in their own towns.

According to their site, their service keeps more than 300 tons *a day* out of landfills! To find and join a local Freecycle group, go to www. freecycle.org.

☐ For great tips on how to have a profitable yard sale, visit www. yardsalequeen. com.

☐ If you'd rather give than sell, you can donate items to your local charity thrift store. Even then, be sure to get a receipt for your donation, because it's tax-deductible. For information on deducting charitable contributions, go to www.irs.gov/ taxtopics/tc506. html.

Pay as You Throw

THE AMAZING TRUTH IS THAT, DEPENDING ON WHERE you live, **75 to 90 percent of your waste can be recycled**. Things that can't be collected through curbside recycling—such as electronics, paints, and batteries—may still be recyclable at a local drop-off center.

Recycling is a special responsibility here in America, where we produce more than a *third* of the world's garbage: 4.5 pounds of trash per person every day. More than half of it ends up in landfills, where it emits more methane—a greenhouse gas—than any other source. Eventually, those landfills leak toxic materials into the surrounding soil and water.

SAVE
an average of $26 a year by "paying as you throw."

PAYT
keeps 6.5 million tons of waste from landfills annually.

Luckily, there's a new trend known as pay-as-you-throw (PAYT). PAYT programs charge residents a fee (between $1 and $2) for each bag or can of waste. So garbage collection gets treated like electricity, gas, and other utilities—you pay for what you use. It's a great incentive to recycle more, compost more, and buy items with less packaging—and save money.

GO GREEN ACTION STEPS

☐ Recycle everything you can. Learn your community's recycling program. To find recycling programs in your area, visit www.earth911.org.

Pay as you throw. According to the EPA, more than 7,000 communities nationwide have PAYT garbage programs in place—and that number is growing. If your community doesn't yet offer a PAYT program, ask your town planner or local elected representatives to visit www.epa.gov, where they can click on "Waste" in the Quick Finder, then select "Pay as You Throw."

Manufacturers are becoming more aware that customers don't want products wrapped in materials like Styrofoam and nonrecyclable plastic (60 percent of which ends up in landfills!). Reward the do-gooders (such as Celestial Seasonings, which uses biodegradeable plastic wrap and doesn't put tags on its tea bags, saving tons of paper and staples) by looking for products that use the least amount of packaging.

Trash Fact

The aluminum cans we throw away each year use up the equivalent of 16 million barrels of oil, enough to fuel a million cars for a year.

GO GREEN
ACTION STEPS

Get Rid of Junk Mail

IN AMERICA, SHOPPING IS A LEISURE ACTIVITY. WE don't even have to leave our homes. Every day, catalogs and junk mail fill our mailboxes with temptation to buy things we don't need. In 2006, we bought $160 billion in merchandise from catalogs. Recycling your catalogs without reading them is one of the easiest ways to get rich (or at least not get poor!) by recycling.

SAVE

$1,413 per year on catalog purchases.

Together, **WE ALL SAVE** *100 million trees a year.*

According to Catalog Choice, more than 8 million tons of trees are used each year to produce 19 billion catalogs, requiring enough energy to power 1.2 million homes for a year and producing as many emissions as 2 million cars. They're then sent to consumers via plane and truck, burning up fossil fuels and adding to global warming. Sears alone sends out more than 425 million catalogs a year—that's nearly a catalog and a half for every single person in the country.

As for junk mail, the average adult is on at least 50 mailing lists, resulting in about 40 pounds of mail sent our way each year. And we forward nearly half of it to the landfill unopened. (Recycle it!)

Luckily, "opt out" legislation now provides web sites and phone numbers that let you just say no to junk mail and catalogs.

GO GREEN ACTION STEPS

☐ Cancel your catalogs. Most catalog mailers use the Abacus database, so taking yourself off the list helps eliminate many catalogs at once. Go to www.abacus-us.com and click on "Consumer Opt-Out."

A new web site, Catalog Choice, lets you opt out of catalog mailing lists individually. Sign up at www.catalogchoice.org, and then each time you receive a catalog you don't want, enter its name into the site's database and decline it.

☐ Cut down on junk mail (fliers and envelopes, rather than catalogs). Call 888-5OPTOUT.

☐ Decline unsolicited credit card offers. Go to www.optoutprescreen.com.

MAKE GREEN
A FAMILY VALUE

AS A FINANCIAL COACH, I'VE HAD THE PLEASURE of working with many families over the years to help them spend less money. One of the most amazing things I've witnessed is how families grow closer as a result of changing their consumption.

One of the gifts of going green is that it can actually change the way we interact with our families. Try this: For the next family birthday, don't just buy more stuff. Instead, spend the day together. Take a trip to a museum or nature preserve. Go for a long bike ride. Cook a meal together. Visit a local farm.

Create traditions together. Maybe every fall you pick apples; every Sunday night you take a long walk; every spring you take a bike trip.

Our choices about how to raise our children have a ripple effect, because they shape the decisions they will make when they grow up and have families.

Today, decide to make green a family value. Read on to learn how.

Green Your Baby

THE BIGGEST—AND STICKIEST—ISSUE WITH RAISING a green baby is what to do about diapers—disposable or cloth?

The National Association of Diaper Services reports that 18 billion disposable diapers are thrown in landfills each year—making up about 2 percent of the garbage in landfills and taking hundreds of years or more to decompose. What's more, disposables cost parents $2,400 during the baby's first two and a half years.

SAVE

$40 a week by nursing.

SAVE

the glass in 600 jars by pureeing your own baby food.

Cloth diapers cost less—especially if you launder them yourself—but in terms of "impact" they're not necessarily better on the environment, thanks to the water and detergent used to clean them. It turns out that diapers are a matter of personal choice. If you do opt for cloth, be sure to use biodegradable, phosphate-free detergent.

Here are some cost-saving baby ideas that are also green:

- Scout out gently used baby clothes at garage sales and consignment shops, and on Craigslist, eBay, and Freecycle.
- Make your own food instead of buying all those

☐ If you choose disposable diapers, be sure to buy the greenest ones available, such as Nature Boy & Girl, which are made with cornstarch instead of plastic (www.natureboy andgirl.net). Or try Seventh Generation's, which are made without chlorine (www. seventhgeneration. com).

☐ To locate a cloth diaper service in your area, visit www.diapernet. org/locate.htm. Another cloth diaper option is the new gDiapers. They're made of cloth but use flushable, biodegradable inserts. Costs are comparable to those of disposable diapers, but these diapers are better for the environment. Visit www. gDiapers.com.

☐ Make your own baby food. Find recipes for easy, all-natural baby food at www. wholesomebaby food.com.

Another important green baby issue has to do with the furniture in your nursery. Some scientists believe that crib death may actually be caused by flame-retardant chemicals—called PBDEs—in beds and mattresses, which become poisonous when they interact with common household fungi. Keep your baby safe by choosing organic, chemical-free mattresses and bedding. For all-natural crib mattresses, visit the web site of manufacturer Hastens at www.hastens.com.

little glass jars. Pureeing vegetables is quick, simple, healthy, and more cost-effective.

- Nurse your baby instead of feeding formula. You'll save about $40 a week, it's healthier, and there's no manufacturing, packaging, or shipping involved.

Green Your Pet

**GO GREEN
ACTION STEPS**

MOST OF US FEEL OUR PETS ARE PART OF THE FAMILY. The greenest choice you can make when it comes to your pet is to "rescue" one from your local shelter, where it might otherwise become one of the 3 to 4 million homeless dogs and cats euthanized every year. Adoption fees are usually around $50 (often a tax-deductible donation), compared to the hundreds of dollars you'd pay a breeder or pet shop.

SAVE
$650 by adopting a pet.

RESCUE
one of 3 to 4 million hopeful dogs or cats.

A big part of going green with our pets involves the food choices we make for them. Many common pet food brands are made with the lowest-quality ingredients, often made overseas with little oversight. This means poor nutrition for your pet, or worse, serious health problems—even death.

Look to save money in other ways in order to save up for better-quality food. In 2006, we spent $38.4 billion on our pets, and there are lower-cost, greener solutions for much of what we buy. Like kids' toys, many pet toys are mass-produced using potentially harmful materials. And chances are you've already got great pet toys at home—like Fido's all-time favorite, the tennis ball.

☐ Adopt a pet. The web site at www.petfinder.com lists animals for adoption at shelters around the country. Or visit www.hsus.org/pets or www.aspca.org or your local animal shelter.

☐ Feed your pet well. Look for brands containing all-natural, whole foods and ingredients—not meat "by-products" and "fillers" made from corn. Avoid foods made with meat "meals," which are leftover animal parts, boiled and processed. Other ingredients in pet food are grown using toxic pesticides or contain potentially hazardous synthetic preservatives, or are made from foods declared unsafe for human consumption. There are dozens of great natural brands to choose from, including Wellness, Innova, Solid Gold, California Natural, and Pinnacle. Visit www.naturapet.com or www.onlynaturalpet.com to learn more about your pet's nutritional needs.

☐ Buy fewer, healthier toys. Look for those made from pesticide-free cotton or recycled materials like fleece and rubber. Get the lowdown on many planet-friendly pet products at www.greatgreenpet.com.

☐ Earth Dog (www.earthdog.com) makes pet products that are good for your best friend and for the planet. All products, including collars, beds, and toys, are made in the United States out of sustainably grown hemp.

Get Outdoors

WHILE IT SOMETIMES SEEMS AS THOUGH WE'VE paved over most of the world, in fact nearly a third of the land in the United States—almost 700 million acres—is owned by the public and managed by various agencies in part for outdoor recreation. We've got urban parks, dense forests, alpine meadows, desert canyons, and remote wilderness.

Let's not only save the earth. Let's get out there and enjoy it.

SAVE
$600 on a gym membership a year.

SUPPORT
the 700 million acres of public lands instead.

Hiking, running, brisk walking, swimming, and bike riding are all activities that require a minimal investment in gear, keep you fit, and get you outside appreciating and reconnecting with nature. Doing these things from your front door saves fuel and greenhouse gas emissions.

Another plus: With the average cost of a gym membership running about $50 a month, moving your workout outdoors can save about $600 a year.

Take the whole family. Childhood expert Richard Louv wrote a thoughtful book called *Last Child in the Woods* (2006), in which he laments that today's kids are "alienated" from nature. He thinks depression, anxiety, and obesity can all be lessened by reacquainting our kids with the grand outdoors.

GO GREEN ACTION STEPS

☐ Take advantage of nearby parks and nature trails. To find a trail close to you, use GORP's Trail Finder at www.gorp.away.com/gorp/trailfinder. At www.publiclands.org, learn about public lands near you and around the country.

☐ Consider participating in a group hike or backpacking trip. Your local chapter of the Sierra Club is a good place to look for group activities. Go to www.sieraclub.com and select your state under "My Backyard" at the top of the page. Retail stores that sell outdoor gear, such as REI, may also offer group activities or have community bulletin boards.

☐ Join a running club in your area at www.running.timeoutdoors.com or www.runningnetwork.com.

☐ Find federally managed public lands near you. Visit these sites:

● **Bureau of Land Management** (www.blm.gov)

● **USDA Forest Service** (www.fs.fed.us)

● **National Park Service** (www.nps.gov)

● **U.S. Bureau of Reclamation** (lakes and reservoirs) (www.usbr.gov)

☐ Find a state park by searching on Google for "state parks" and the name of your state.

☐ Once you've gotten into the outdoors habit, quit the gym.

Green Your Holidays

BELIEVE IT OR NOT, AMERICANS SPEND $2.7 BILLION every year on gift wrap. It's insane! That's more than the entire gross domestic product (GDP) of many countries in Africa and Asia. One easy way to green your holidays is to stop buying nonrecyclable wrapping paper printed with petroleum-based inks and dyes.

We'd **ALL SAVE** *$2.6 billion by getting creative with wrapping each year.*

We'd **ALL SAVE** *300,000 trees by buying recycled cards, too.*

Use gift wrap made out of recycled paper—or better yet, use materials around your home to dress up your packages. When I was a kid, my creative mom used the Sunday comics. It looked cool and didn't cost a dime.

Next, green your greetings. Nearly 300,000 trees are harvested each year to produce all the holiday cards sold in the United States—enough to fill a football field 10 stories high! Save money, time, and trees by sending free e-cards instead of traditional cards. Or opt to order from Cards for Causes (www.cardsforcauses.com) or Good Cause Greetings (www.goodcausegreetings.com), where not only are the cards made of recycled paper, but 10 or 20 percent of the purchase price goes to the charity of your choice.

And finally, give eco-friendly gifts. Give a gift you can't wrap, like a charity donation in someone's name.

☐ Shop for recyclable gift wrap at sites like: www.papermojo.com.

www.paporganics.com.

www.eartheasy.com.

☐ Send a free e-card. Visit: www.hallmark.com.

www.AmericanGreetings.com.

www.bluemountain.com.

☐ Give green gifts. For dozens of ideas—from a National Parks Pass to a donation to the Fresh Air Fund in someone's name—check out the NRDC's Great Green Gift-Giving Guide. Go to www.nrdc.org and click on "Green Living." You'll find the "Giving Green Gifts" link in the "Green Living Toolkit."

Another gift idea: Many conservation groups have sponsorship programs, where you can "adopt" a particular species—polar bears, sea turtles, penguins—to help protect it. Visit the "Wildlife Adoption Center" at www.worldwildlife.org.

☐ Don't forget to "tree-cycle" after the holidays. Go to www.earth911.org to learn how.

Have a Green Christmas

with a real tree. The National Christmas Tree Association reports that most artificial trees are made of PVC—a potential source of hazardous lead. (That's why they come with a warning label!) But real trees are a renewable, recyclable resource. The best choice is one that's sustainably grown and pesticide-free.

Take a Volunteer Vacation

IMAGINE YOU AND YOUR FAMILY, OFF ON A SCIENtific expedition, like studying whales in British Columbia or helping manage a rain forest in Puerto Rico.

VACATION
for as little as $20 plus travel expenses.

The memories:
PRICELESS.

Next year, instead of going to a seaside resort or to an amusement park, plan to take your family on a volunteer vacation. You'll save money, have a terrific adventure, and provide valuable manpower on projects that are helping the planet and all its inhabitants.

Many volunteer vacations are a subset of a booming trend known as "ecotourism." That means environmentally conscious travel to places where nature is the main attraction. Many of the places where nature is at its most dramatic are in less developed countries, so ecotourism also aims to benefit the people who live there—by using local services (for example, hiring guides or eating in restaurants) and by helping protect the place you're visiting. While there are an increasing number of high-end eco-resorts, there are also many inexpensive opportunities to stay in com-

☐ Research the various volunteer vacation options. In addition to Sierra Club and WWOOF, try these:

● **Habitat for Humanity**, at www.habitat.org, runs domestic and international trips to help build affordable housing.

● **Earthwatch Institute**, at www.earthwatch.org, offers opportunities for families to help out on scientific expeditions, like studying whales in British Columbia or helping manage a rain forest in Puerto Rico.

fort surrounded by spectacular scenery—especially if you're willing to volunteer your time.

In addition to the specific project you're working on, there's usually a lot more to enjoy: the company and camaraderie of fellow volunteers; the travel to spectacular locales; meeting, working, and living with local folks; and spending your time off exploring the area.

The Sierra Club offers an amazing selection of "service trips" in the United States, Canada, and overseas. Trips range in price from $395 to $5,000. In most instances, food and lodging are included—as are some transportation costs. Care to enjoy spring in the Sierras while working to refurbish and rebuild campground picnic tables in Yosemite National Park? Or is whale watching in Maui more your style? Visit www.sierraclub.org and search on "volunteer vacations."

A truly inexpensive option can be found through World-Wide Opportunities on Organic Farms (WWOOF), an international network of more than 600 host farms in the United States—including Hawaii and the U.S. Virgin Islands. Each farm welcomes travelers in exchange for volunteer time working on the farm. Your only expenses are a registration fee of $20 and travel costs to and from the farm. Pick grapes in California's beautiful wine country or learn about organic gardening in the splendor of the Southern Colorado Rockies. Visit www.wwoofusa.org for more details.

- **Global Volunteers**, at www.globalvolunteers.org, offers programs around the world, from helping provide health care in Ghana to teaching English in Poland.

- **Travelocity**, at www.travelocity.com/travelforgood, has created a whole mini-site to help plan volunteer vacations.

☐ Once you've narrowed down your choices, find out exactly what kind of project you'll be working on, what's provided and what you must bring, and what particular skills or qualifications you need. Whenever possible, get references from previous volunteers.

☐ For ecotourism without volunteer requirements, try these resources:

- **The International Ecotourism Society** unites communities, conservation, and sustainable travel. Visit www.ecotourism.org.

- **The Worldwide Fund for Nature** has eco-travel tips at www.panda.org. Click on "Travel Smart." WWF also offers eco-trips throughout North America, Asia, Africa, the South Pacific, and even Antarctica. Research trips or download the travel guide at www.worldwildlife.org/travel.

- **The Rainforest Alliance** explains the principles and importance of ecotourism, offers tips for travelers, and offers listings of sustainable hotels, tour operators, and other tourism businesses through its Eco-Index for Latin America and the Caribbean.

Visit the web site at www.rainforest-alliance.org, then click on "Tourism." The Eco-Index is at www.eco-indextourism.org/en/home.

- **Conservation International's** (CI's) ecotourism site has a list of places to stay that were developed with help from CI—like an eco-lodge in a Bolivian national park. Visit www.ecotour.org and click on "Destinations."

GO GREEN AT WORK

MANY OF US ARE LEARNING TO BE GREEN at home. But at work it is easy to slip into some destructive habits.

A 2007 poll commissioned by Sun Microsystems, Inc., and conducted by Harris Interactive reveals that the majority of employees don't even do the simple things to help their employers conserve energy. Only 42 percent of workers turn off the lights and only 34 percent turn off their computers when work is done.

But consider the following: If those workers *did* turn off the lights and their computers (or if the network were set to do so for them), $4.3 billion in energy costs would be saved along with 32 million tons of CO_2 emissions.

This may be just your opportunity to pave the way. Show the boss how green improvements can make a positive impact on the office—and increase the bottom line—and you could ultimately earn yourself a reputation for innovation. You might even get a raise.

If you own your own business, going green reduces your costs and, according to a November 2007 *Wall Street Journal* article, even attracts young talent. A recent poll on MonsterTrak.com found that 80 percent of young professionals are interested in securing a job that has a positive impact on the environment, and 92 percent would be more inclined to work for a company that is environmentally friendly.

An environmentally friendly workplace also has a huge impact on employee productivity. The Lawrence Berkeley National Laboratory in Berkeley, California, conducted a study that found that, in the United States alone, the estimated potential annual savings and productivity gains from better indoor environments are $6–$14 billion from reduced respiratory disease, $1–$4 billion from reduced allergies and asthma, $10–$30 billion from reduced "sick building syndrome" symptoms, and $20–$160 billion from direct improvements in worker performance unrelated to health. Amazing.

Going green is a win-win for any savvy employer and employee.

GO GREEN
ACTION STEPS

☐ Visit my web site at www. finishrich.com and click on "Latte Factor Calculator" on the bottom of the home page. Plug in the amount of money you are spending on takeout lunches and figure out

Bring Your Lunch to Work

FOR YEARS MY GRANDMOTHER ROSE BACH brownbagged her lunch when she worked at Gimbels department store. She invested the money she saved from not eating out and became a millionaire. Her story is the inspiration for every book I've written.

SAVE

$2,250 a year by brown-bagging your lunch.

Together, we'll **REDUCE** *our landfills by 1.8 million tons of trash.*

The very first Latte Factor was the Brown Bag Factor!

Today, Americans spend over $134 billion a year on fast food. While it's convenient, it's not always cheap (or healthy). Let's say you spend $9 every day on a chicken sandwich and a soda at your local Subway. That's $45 a week—and $2,250 a year! If you were to save that amount every year and invest it instead, in 20 years you'd have more than $111,000!

But apart from your health and wealth, takeout food packaging is a huge waste of resources. When I walk down the streets of New York at lunchtime, nearly everyone I pass is carrying plastic-wrapped food and plastic utensils in a white plastic bag. ***Takeout food packaging creates 1.8 million tons of trash in the United States every year.*** The alternative? Bring your lunch.

the small fortune you'll save by brown-bagging it.

☐ Bring your lunch in a reusable bag.

☐ Get creative. For yummy "brown-bag" lunches (which you should now rename "reusable bag" lunches), try www. fabulousfoods. com. The list of ideas is intended for kids' lunch boxes, but with items like pesto pasta salad and goat cheese sandwiches with roasted peppers and fresh basil, they're perfect for adult lunches, too. You can also find great quick lunch recipes at www. cooks.com.

☐ Retire at the beach. My grandmother Rose's friends at Gimbels teased her for being so "cheap." She ultimately laughed her way to the beaches of California, where she retired (while her friends retired and stayed in Milwaukee, Wisconsin—much colder).

In New Jersey, one study found that roughly a quarter of all litter comes from takeout food packaging, second only to cigarette butts. Another example of how your Latte Factor becomes your Litter Factor!

Green Your Computer

IF EVERY U.S. COMPUTER AND MONITOR WERE turned off at night, the nation could shut down eight large power stations and avoid emitting 7 million tons of CO_2 every year. It's that easy.

Even when your computer is on, you can make a difference. According to the Environmental Protection Agency, only about 5 percent of laptop and desktop computers used in the United States have their energy efficiency settings enabled. The power-management features of most computer brands and operating systems can be accessed by going to Settings and opening the Control Panel and clicking on "Power Options." Search the dialogue box for references to "low power mode," "sleep mode," "hibernate," or "standby." The EPA estimates that enabling these settings can help conserve as much as 80 percent of the energy that would have been consumed otherwise.

SAVE *your company millions of dollars in electricity costs.*

Together, we could **SHUT DOWN** *eight large power stations.*

GO GREEN ACTION STEPS

☐ Shut your computer down at night. If you work in an office, speak to your managers about setting up the network to do it automatically.

☐ Enable your computer's power-efficiency settings. Snap.com offers a software program

A recent article on GreenerComputing.com reports that General Electric saved $6.5 million in electricity costs a year simply by changing its computers' settings.

called CO_2 saver. This lightweight program manages your computer's power usage when it's idle, saving energy and decreasing the demand on your power utility. Download it for free at www.co2saver.snap.com.

☐ Don't rush to buy a new computer. For advice on when to buy a new desktop computer versus when to upgrade your existing model, green ratings for a variety of PCs, and recycling information, go to Consumer Reports' Greener Choices web site at www.greenerchoices.org and click on "Electronics."

☐ Recycle old computers. To find out how to recycle electronics in your state, go to www.eiae.org. The site also has a list of questions to ask potential recyclers, so you'll know your computer is being recycled responsibly. Much of our electronic waste is simply shipped to India and China, where there is little waste regulation and where toxic materials like mercury, lead, and PVC are polluting the environment.

☐ Take an hour this week to set up your bills online. Call your bank or log on to their web site. Most large banks—and even many smaller ones—now offer free online bill payment to customers who enroll in online banking.

The following are some other online bill-paying services: www.my checkfree.com

www.paytrust.com

www.myezbills. com

www.quicken.com

☐ Get a free 30-day trial of The Automatic Money Manager, an online tool that my team and I developed with Finicity. It's a great way to not only pay your bills but automate all of your finances. Go to www. automaticmoney manager.com.

Do It Online

GO GREEN IN YOUR HOME OFFICE, TOO. PAYING BILLS online is simply a no-brainer. It saves you time and money, saves millions of trees from being clear-cut and used for paper, and saves companies money— savings that may eventually be passed along to you.

Here are the facts. If all U.S. households received electronic statements instead of paper, and paid their bills online, collectively we'd save 18.5 million trees every year, enough wood for more than 216,000 houses; 2.2 billion tons of carbon dioxide and other greenhouse gases; and 1.7 billion pounds of solid waste.

SAVE
$400 or more on stamps and late fees.

Collectively we can **SPARE** *18.5 million trees.*

Many of the companies you do business with—for your credit cards, cell phones, cable TV, utilities, and so on— will offer you the option to receive an electronic statement. Once you access it (via email or logging in to your payee's web site), you can pay electronically—either through an online bill-pay service, through your online bank account, or directly through the payee.

Having payments *automatically* drawn from your checking or savings account ensures that you'll never miss a payment and never rack up a late fee—saving you from a few dollars to more than a hundred dollars a month.

Consider reading your newspapers online as well. The *New York Times* costs about $330 a year for home delivery (outside New York City), but all content is free online. For $14.95 a month (slightly more than half the newsprint delivery price), you can subscribe to an online edition that looks exactly like the print edition—minus the dead trees.

Think Before You Print

Do you *really* need a hard copy? At Finish Rich Media, we've added a message below our corporate email signatures, reminding recipients to think twice before printing an email.

The Environmental Energy Technologies Division of the U.S. government reports that the average American office worker uses about 10,000 sheets of paper—a stack four feet high— every year.

SAVE

.6 cents for every sheet of paper you don't buy.

SPARE THE AIR

18 to 60 pounds of pollution for every 40 cases of recycled paper in your office.

According to the Natural Resources Defense Council (www.nrdc.org), the pulp and paper industry may contribute to more global and local environmental problems than any other industry in the world—razing trees, polluting waterways, and destroying wildlife habitat. Mills that use virgin timber generate hazardous air pollutants, including dioxins and other cancer-causing chemicals.

Paper accounts for more than a third of all municipal waste—more than any other material. American offices send 4 million tons of paper to the landfill every year.

Could you just as easily deal with any of your documents electronically?

GO GREEN ACTION STEPS

☐ Think before you print.

☐ If you have a double-sided printer or copier, set the default to print on both sides of the paper.

☐ Buy only recycled. The higher the recycled content, the better. Virtually every paper company and office supply store chain now sells recycled options. Look for the word

According to the Natural Resources Defense Council, buying 40 cases of copy paper made from 30 percent postconsumer paper instead of paper made from virgin pulp saves more than seven trees, 2,100 gallons of water, 1,230 kilowatt-hours of electricity, and 18 pounds of air pollution. The same amount of paper made from 100 percent postconsumer paper saves 24 trees, 7,000 gallons of water, 4,100 kilowatt-hours of electricity, and 60 pounds of air pollution!

"postconsumer," meaning the product is recycled from paper used by offices or consumers, and look for the green recycled logo on the package. Visit www.greenhome. com for a great selection of recycled office supplies, everything from recycled paper to recycled Post-it notes, recycled file folders—even recycled paper clips!

☐ The Natural Resources Defense Council has helpful resources for businesses that want to implement a "smart paper program." Access their toolkit at www.nrdc.org/ greenliving and click on the "Smart Paper" link. While you're there, read about businesses that are saving money and resources by changing the way they buy and use paper.

☐ Recycle what you use. If your building doesn't have a recycling program in place, check www. earth911.com for a recycling service in your area. Consider joining with other businesses in your building or office block to get better recycling services at a lower cost.

☐ Use remanufactured printer cartridges. According to www.ehow.

com, one-third of businesses nationwide do. Check the instructions in the box of your new laser or inkjet cartridge to find out how to recycle your old one. Many companies will provide instructions, packaging materials, and free postage if you wish to recycle your old cartridge, which is then refilled and used again.

Telecommute

MORE PEOPLE ARE WORKING FROM HOME THAN EVER before in this country. Employers and employees alike are reaping the rewards—and it's great for the environment!

According to the report "Telework Trendlines" by WorldatWork (www.workingfromanywhere.org), the number of Americans whose employer permitted them to work from home at least one day per month increased to 12.4 million in 2006, up from about 9.9 million in 2005.

SAVE

$215 on commuting annually by working one day a week from home.

REDUCE

the 95,000 tons of perc that is released by dry cleaners into the environment each year in the United States and Canada.

By telecommuting just two days per week, over the course of a year an employee will drive 3,000 fewer miles, save approximately $430 in gas, and eliminate 3,120 pounds of CO_2 emissions.

The benefits to an employee include more flexibility, commuting money saved, less stress, and overall increased satisfaction in his or her job. Employers can reduce office space and operating expenses, and benefit from lower employee absenteeism, lower turnover, and increased employee productivity.

If telecommuting can work with the job you do, prepare your case well and ask your employer for a trial program.

☐ Prepare your case for telecommuting. For suggestions on how to present your proposal, read "Making Your Case for Telecommuting" at www. quintcareers.com/ telecommuting_ options.html. For research to support your case, go to the nonprofit Telework Coalition's web site, www.telcoa.org.

☐ Find jobs that allow you to work from home. For ideas, consult www. ratracerebellion. com.

If you dress for the office, telecommuting could save you plenty on your yearly dry-cleaning bill. And less dry cleaning is also good for the planet. Dry cleaning uses perchloroethylene, or perc, a toxic chemical that's harmful to the environment and potentially carcinogenic. When you do need to use a dry cleaner, go green. To find a green dry cleaner in your area, visit www.greenearthcleaning.com or check your local Yellow Pages. In the past year, I switched to Green Apple Cleaners (www. greenapplecleaners.com) in New York City, and I absolutely love their service.

Be a Green Business Traveler

AIR TRAVEL ACCOUNTS FOR LESS THAN 5 PERCENT of human-caused carbon dioxide emissions—but it's also growing more quickly than any other emissions source. From 1990 to 2004, the amount of CO_2 emissions due to air travel doubled. Emissions from U.S. aircraft are expected to increase by 65 percent by 2025, and triple by 2050.

SAVE *up to $200 by taking the train.*

HELP *a hotel save 6,000 gallons of water a month by reusing your linens.*

As if that weren't enough, high altitude also exacerbates the impacts of two other greenhouse gases emitted by burning jet fuel—nitrogen oxide and water vapor.

More than 18 percent of air travel is for business purposes. Yet surely much of it is easily avoidable by making use of today's new technologies, such as video teleconferencing.

When you must travel, seek out airlines that are making their business more sustainable. Continental (www.continental.com) has taken the lead among U.S. airlines: It spent more than $16 billion over the last

decade to upgrade its fleet with more fuel-efficient planes. It also installed devices on the wings of some older planes that reduce emissions by 5 percent. Continental has 13 full-time staffers working on reducing the resource use and emissions of all its operations, as well as designing greener terminals.

In Europe, Virgin Atlantic (www.virginatlantic.com) is experimenting with using biofuels in its jets, and

GO GREEN
ACTION STEPS
....

☐ Whenever pos-
sible, choose to fly
with airlines that
are making sus-
tainable decisions.
Look on their web
sites for informa-
tion about their
environmental
initiatives.

☐ Try to fly less,
or fly shorter
distances. For
every mile you fly,
roughly .6 pounds
of CO_2 is emitted.

☐ Opt for
direct flights if
they don't cost
more—taking off
and landing are
a plane's most
fuel-intensive
maneuvers.

also aiming to reduce its emissions by using fewer engines for takeoff. A European Union plan to require carbon reductions from all airlines that fly through EU countries could have a big impact in the next few years.

You can also seek out greener hotels. Many hotels—big and small—have begun making sustainability a part of their service. Marriott (www.marriott.com) is the industry leader as far as chains go, with a program to reduce its emissions by one million tons as well as to conserve water, reduce waste, and build environmentally friendly hotels. The following are some of the programs that are part of Marriott's long-standing commitment to the environment:

- **The Linen Reuse Program**, which encourages guests to reuse towels and linens, saves an average of 11 to 17 percent on hot water and sewer costs at each hotel.
- **The "Re-lamp" Campaign**, which replaced 450,000 lightbulbs with CFLs in 2006, saved 65 percent on lighting costs and energy usage in guest rooms.
- **The replacement of 400,000 showerheads** with low-flow alternatives, reducing use of hot water by 10 percent each year.

Doubletree has also gotten into the game. The company's Portland hotel (www.doubletreeportlandgreen.com) has significantly reduced water and energy use, buys wind energy, buys the majority of its food from local sources, and even composts its kitchen waste.

☐ For shorter trips, consider taking the train. It can save you money, cut down on endless airport hassles, and significantly reduce your carbon emissions. It might even save you time: Consider those airport security lines and all-too-common flight delays. If you're traveling between Washington, D.C., New York, and Boston, Amtrak's Metroliner service costs slightly less than a flight—roughly $138 versus $164. Amtrak's service between Los Angeles and San Diego can save you up to $200 (the train fare is $58, compared to about $258 for a flight). Before booking short-distance flights (such as those that last an hour or less), check your train options at www.amtrak.com.

☐ Search for a green hotel at www.environmentallyfriendlyhotels.com and www.greenhotels.com/members.htm.

☐ Opt not to have your towels and sheets washed daily during your stay. Many hotels now offer towel and linen reuse programs. According to Project Planet (www.projectplanetcorp.com), in one month a 100-room hotel can save 6,000 gallons of water and 40 gallons of detergent, and also save money on labor, electricity, and linen-replacement fees. The average hotel can save more than $20,000 in its first year of implementing the program.

☐ When you do fly, bring a reusable water bottle that you can fill at a water fountain once you've cleared security, and pack your own food to make less trash.

☐ The next time you need a car service, think green with OZOextra Network. Find a green car service in your area by visiting www.ozocar.com.

FINISH RICH:
MAKE YOUR FIRST
GREEN MILLION

THROUGHOUT THIS BOOK, I'VE SHOWN YOU ways to save money by living a greener lifestyle, and for each of those ways there are companies offering products and services to help you go green. From green dry cleaners to manufacturers of biodegradeable makeup, there are people launching businesses making or selling products no one even knew they wanted just a few years ago. From hotel chains to office-supply stores, even companies that seem to have been around forever are deep into "green initiatives."

In the introduction, I stated that *I believe green investing will be to the twenty-first century what technology was to the twentieth century.* Green investing is simple—it's about investing in opportunities, companies, and services that will both support and promote climate change in an effort to reduce CO_2 output, improve the environment, and turn the tide on global warming.

The financial consequences of a changing climate and the global crisis it is presenting are staggering in their implications for our corporations and consumers. Those that change and adapt to become "eco-conscious" will financially flourish— and those that don't may be financially devastated. This may sound dramatic, but the fact is that companies are already dedicating BILLIONS annually to becoming eco-friendly. And many of these companies are quickly returning billions to the bottom line as a result. *In the future, "going green" may permeate every single financial decision that impacts your family's financial life.*

The financial services industry is rapidly tuning in to the global opportunities and financial profits that exist in the green space. They are investing billions in companies in the space and already packaging investment banking, financing, and credit products around "green eco-conscious opportunities." That means you don't have to start from scratch, researching every investment opportunity individually. Fund managers are creating mutual funds you can easily invest in, and invest-

ment banks are creating new "indexes" so you can easily know which stocks pass environmental muster. It is getting easier every day to borrow, invest, spend, and earn in ways that are better for the planet.

If you are not already investing for your future, I hope that this little book will convince you that you can afford to do so. In the 40-some tips you've read until now, surely you have found one or two that you can take action on?

The secret to turning small daily savings into huge future returns are two basic principles that I've discussed in other books. The first principle, called "Pay Yourself First," means using your 401(k) plan, or a similar plan that you may have through your employer, to make small contributions with every paycheck. In other words, you don't wait until the end of the month to see what you have "left over" to save. Let's face it. There is never anything left over! Pay Yourself First means paying for your future BEFORE you pay your bills, BEFORE you even pay your taxes.

The beauty of a 401(k) plan is that the government allows you to save money up to $15,500 in 2008* without paying a dime to the government first. For much more on 401(k) plans and retirement investing, read my book *The Automatic Millionaire*. You can read it in less than two hours and learn everything you need to know about saving for your future, more than I can cover in detail here. Go to www.AutomaticMillion aire.com to download a free chapter.

A 401(k) plan through your employer also makes it easy to save *automatically*, and that is the second basic principle of getting rich on an

---

* In 2008, the maximum allowable contribution for a 401(k) plan is $15,500. If you're over 50, you can make an additional "catch up" contribution of $5,000. After 2008, increases will be adjusted for inflation in $500 increments.

ordinary income: "Make It Automatic." With a 401(k) plan, you set your contribution in the form of a percentage of your salary (your company's human resources representative will show you how) and that percentage is deducted from every paycheck automatically. It works like those slow cookers do: You simply "fix it and forget it."

If you don't have a 401(k) plan, you can easily set up an IRA through almost any bank or mutual fund company. An IRA gives you the same opportunity as a 401(k) plan to invest with "pretax" dollars. In 2008, the maximum is $5,000 a year.* With an IRA, you have the option to write a single check for the entire amount at one time, but it is actually better to contribute over time. You can set up your IRA to withdraw a certain amount of money from your checking or savings account automatically each week or two weeks, timed for when you get paid. That way, once again you don't have to hope that there is money "left over" to invest, and you also benefit from the highs and lows of the market (what is known as dollar-cost averaging). And with an IRA, you get to deduct your contributions on your tax return.

Either way, your new green daily savings will be set up to move tax-free into a richer future for you and your family.

With either a 401(k) plan or an IRA, the next step after you set it up is to choose the investments that your money will be used to purchase. That is where today's green investing opportunities make things exciting. In the next tip, you will learn how to catch the wave of green investing. It is the very best way that you can "save the earth and get rich trying." Read on.

---

* In 2008, the maximum allowable contribution for an IRA is $5,000. If you're over 50, you can make an additional "catch up" contribution of $1,000. After 2008, increases will be adjusted for inflation in $500 increments.

Invest Green

GREEN INVESTING IS FINALLY COMING INTO ITS OWN, WHICH IS GREAT news for the environment—and your ability to build wealth.

The concept of "socially responsible investing," called SRI for short, has been around for decades and is now becoming increasingly popular—it already has $2.3 trillion invested in it. SRI started out by appealing to investors who wanted to avoid "sin stocks," the stocks of companies that are involved in alcohol, tobacco, gambling, and so forth. Today, SRI has evolved, and the new focus by consumers, business, and government on sustainability and the environment has created its own category of SRI.

As with all financial trends, Wall Street is getting there first before "Main Street." Goldman Sachs has already set aside $1.5 billion to privately invest in green companies. CalPERS and CalSTRS (California's teacher retirement pension plan—one of the largest institutional investors in the country) have set aside more than a billion dollars for green investments.

This is truly just the beginning—so the question really is how to catch this wave. How can you get rich by investing green? The most obvious way to dip your toe into "green investing" is to invest in an SRI, like a socially responsible index fund or an SRI exchange-traded mutual fund (ETF).

One of the largest active money managers of SRI mutual funds is Calvert Funds (www.calvert.com). They offer both index-based and actively managed socially conscious funds. Check out Calvert Large Cap Growth Fund (symbol: CLGAX), which has outperformed the S&P 500 over the last five years.

For ETFs, check out ishares (www.ishares.com). The ishares KLD Select Social Index "screens in" companies that have positive social and environmental characteristics. The ishares KLD 400 Social Index (symbol: DSI) tracks the Domini 400 Social Index, which "screens out" companies involved in alcohol, tobacco, firearms, and gambling, et cetera, and, within those parameters, looks for companies with positive environmental, social, and governance (ESG) performance.

Not all SRI funds are alike. For decades, SRI has screened out companies that were considered socially or ethically unacceptable, like weapons manufacturers, whereas now some SRI funds (and most "green funds") screen in companies that are making a positive impact instead. Today's green funds include some surprising choices. As more and more mainstream companies embrace sustainability as part of good business, blue-chip companies are becoming more common.

There are currently only a handful of "green funds," both mutual funds and exchange-traded mutual funds, but I am confident this will change soon. Some are "clean tech" funds, which invest in companies involved in alternative energy and related technologies. Others use ESG criteria to evaluate companies' impacts on both people and the planet.

Winslow Green Growth (symbol: WGGFX) (www.winslowgreen.com) is annually the best-performing green mutual over five years. This small-growth fund invests in domestic companies that are either in specific green sectors or have shown strong environmental responsibility. The fund was launched in 2001, and its creators are currently about to launch a second green fund, called the Winslow Green Solutions Fund.

The New Alternatives Fund (symbol: NALFX) (www.newalternatives fund.com) was founded in 1982. The fund holds companies—both overtly green and less visibly so—that it believes "have a positive impact on the environment." Many of its holdings are in the renewable-energy space, but it also invests in natural foods companies (like Whole Foods) and those involved in clean water and clean air.

Green Century Funds (www.greencentury.com) currently manages two green funds. Started in 1991, they offer the Green Century Equity Fund (symbol: GCEQX), which seeks to track the Domini 400 Social Index, and the Green Century Balanced Fund (symbol: GCLBX), which includes stocks and bonds of environmentally responsible corporations of various sizes. The fund company is nonprofit and promises that their fees and profits are used to preserve and protect the environment.

In addition to mutual funds, there are now a number of green exchange-traded funds that are doing well and are focused on renewable forms of energy. Morgan Stanley recently put out a research report called "Clean Energy: Sustainable Opportunities." They predict that annual clean-energy revenue opportunities could reach $500 billion by 2020 and a trillion annually by 2030.

One of the largest renewable-energy funds is PowerShares WilderHill Clean Energy (symbol: PBW), which seeks to mirror the Wilder Hill Clean Energy Index. This exchange-traded fund, started in March 2005, focuses on companies that promote cleaner energy. Another PowerShares ETF, Wilder-Hill Progressive Energy Portfolio (PUW), focuses on companies that provide technologies that improve the use of existing fossil fuels. Others include PowerShares Cleantech Portfolio (PZD), Claymore/ LGA Green ETF (GRN), Van Eck Global Alternative Energy ETF (GEX), and First Trust NASDAQ Clean Edge ETF (QCLN).

GO GREEN ACTION STEPS

☐ If you are eligible for a 401(k) plan at work, find out if your investment "menu" includes a green fund. If it doesn't, speak to your plan administrator (usually someone in your company's human resources department) and express your interest in having an SRI or a green fund added to your choices.

☐ Begin researching a few of the funds I've mentioned. As I write this, many of the green funds listed on pages 137 and 138 have posted double-digit returns and many were up tremendously in 2007, some over 30 percent. **This does not mean that you should invest your entire retirement savings in a green fund.** Many of these funds are narrowly focused and volatile. Others are quite broadly diversified. So before you invest, do your research carefully and consider green investing a piece of your overall financial plan and diversification. A great place to start your research is at Morningstar. com, which evaluates funds, their diversification, and their levels of risk.

☐ Sign up for my free green investment alerts at www.greengreen. com. I will be continuing to write on the performance of these green funds and future green investment opportunities. You can register to receive my free green investment alert and be notified the moment I post.

☐ To learn how your current holdings perform in terms of sustainability, there are several tools you can use. Climate Counts (www. climatecounts. org) provides a scorecard for companies in eight sectors based on their commitment to fighting global warming.

☐ Social Investment Forum can help you find a financial planner who specializes in socially responsible investing. Go to www.socialinvest. org and click on "Individual Investors," where you'll find a financial services directory and other tools.

Start a Green Business

IN MY BOOK *START LATE, FINISH RICH*, I WROTE ABOUT how creating a second stream of income can change your life. Every day people are making money in every kind of business imaginable. How about you?

As the world races to find solutions to climate change, dwindling oil supplies, and many other environmental problems, it's creating vast opportunities for entrepreneurs to earn millions while helping protect the planet. In virtually every field—energy, transportation, manufacturing, design, food, health, you name it—there are problems requiring innovative solutions.

Why not come up with one? Pause in whatever you're doing today and ask yourself whether there's a smarter, better, greener way to do it. You might just come up with a million-dollar idea. That's what happened with Adam Lowry and Eric Ryan, cofounders of green cleaning products company Method (www. methodhome.com). Fed up with their dirty house, toxic cleaners, and poorly designed products that get hidden away under the sink, the two built a company to sell nontoxic, biodegradable cleaners in sleek, recycled containers. Seven years later, they ranked seventh on *Inc.* magazine's list of the fastest-growing companies—and their products, sold in stores like Costco and Target, are generating $40 million in annual revenue.

What are you waiting for?

GO GREEN ACTION STEPS

☐ Get inspired by more green entrepreneurs who made good. (A 2006 study commissioned by Shell Springboard, a division of Royal Dutch Shell, concluded that green businesses around the world stand to earn a trillion dollars by 2010!)

Here are some companies worth reading about:

- **Stonyfield Farm**, organic dairy (www.stonyfield.com)

- **TerraCycle**, waste-eliminating garden products company (www.terracycle.net)

- **Method**, green cleaning products (www.methodhome.com)

- **New Belgium**, award-winning sustainable microbrewery (www.newbelgium.com)

- **Pharmaca**, eco-friendly pharmacy (www.pharmaca.com)

- **Whole Foods**, natural foods chain (www.wholefoodsmarket.com)

- **Chipotle**, sustainably-minded fast food (www.chipotle.com)

☐ Consider getting a job or creating a business in the new "green collar" economy. Read about it at www.greenlivingideas.com. Scroll over "Topics" and then over "Work and the Office," and click on "Green Collar Jobs."

Try Green Direct Selling

Maybe you don't have an original green business idea but you're still interested in earning extra income while helping others to go green. Through direct-selling opportunities—also called network marketing—you can own a proven business selling products directly to people rather than in a store.

According to the Direct Selling Association (DSA), more than 15.2 million Americans participated in direct selling in 2006, generating more than $32 billion for their parent companies and themselves.

One of the original green network marketing companies is Shaklee, whose products include a highly touted line of all-natural cleaners that are nontoxic, biodegradable, hypoallergenic, and not tested on animals. According to Shaklee, they were the first company in the world to obtain Climate Neutral certifications totally offsetting their CO_2 emissions. Founded in 1956, Shaklee was "green before green was cool," *Fortune* magazine recently said.

Legitimate direct selling is not a get-rich-quick business, but if you are willing to work hard, it can be a great way to earn extra income.

GO GREEN ACTION STEPS

☐ Read my report titled "Thirteen Reasons to Consider Direct Selling and the Five Things to Look Out For." Log on to www.greengreen.com/directselling.

☐ To learn more about direct selling and direct-selling opportunities, visit the Direct Selling Association at www.dsa.org.

☐ Take some time to explore the green opportunities offered by the companies listed below. *And before you sign up with anyone, be sure to check out their financials and meet their management.*

● **Shaklee Corporation**
(www.shaklee.com) The number-one natural nutrition company in the United States

● **Amazon Herb Company**
(www.rainforest bio.com) Spa and wellness products

● **The Body Shop**
(www.thebodyshop athome.com) Skin care and makeup

● **Happy Soul**
(www.thehap pysoul.com) Spa and aromatherapy products

● **Cleure**
(www.cleure.com) Pure personal-care products

● **OurHouse**
(www.ourhouse works.com) Green home cleaning products

● **The Happy Gardener**
(www.thehappy gardener.info) Organic gardening supplies

● **Daisy Blue Naturals**
(www.daisyblue naturals.com) Natural skin care products

● **Aihu**
(www.aihu.net) Health and healing products

GIVE GREEN

I N MY LAST THREE BOOKS, I'VE SHARED MY thoughts on the importance of giving back. The truth is, the more you give, the more you get back. And the more you give to the Earth, the more the Earth will give back to you. I firmly believe this, and I do my best to follow this advice in my own life. I support and am active with many great charities. With my last book, *The Automatic Millionaire Homeowner,* I donated $120,000 to Habitat For Humanity New York City to build a building for eight families in the Bronx and I joined their board. Habitat New York is leading the push to build green homes for its Habitat families (visit www.habitatnyc.org). Recently, I kicked off the launch of this book by donating $50,000, with Wells Fargo, to Waterkeeper Alliance at the 2007 California Governor and First Lady's Conference on Women.

Waterkeeper Alliance is a grassroots movement of more than 160 Waterkeeper programs on six continents, united in defense of their local water bodies and for global water-resource protection. Many of their local programs find solutions to water scarcity through the law, innovation, and education. Helping your local waterways thrive helps your local economy flourish. To get involved and to support Waterkeeper Alliance, visit www.wa ter keeper.org.

It's our responsibility to preserve the Earth for future generations—for our children and grandchildren to enjoy. Right now there are countless groups working around the globe—even in your own community—to help protect this amazing planet that we call home.

Giving green does not just mean donating money. The world also needs your time and talents—and especially your voice.

Give to a Green Cause

WHILE THERE ARE MANY GREAT ORGANIZATIONS helping in our fight against global warming, I do have a few favorites.

The Alliance for Climate Protection, led by Al Gore, is using scientific facts to educate Americans on the urgency and need for climate-change solutions. Their web site is loaded with resources, from eye-opening statistics to instructions on how to get involved with global movements. You can read more about this organization and how to support their mission at www.climateprotect.org.

One of the oldest and largest groups that use nature as an inspiration to bring people together to protect the planet is the Sierra Club. With chapters across the country and more than 1.3 million members, this is one group you should definitely check out. Visit their web site at www.sierraclub.org to find out how to support your local chapter. You can find outdoor activities taking place in your community, and information on local and state issues that need your voice.

The Natural Resource Defense Council is a key player in helping to protect our home, Earth. Leading lawyers and policy makers ensure that the NRDC stays on the cutting edge of key national and global environmental issues. To donate now and read more about the impact they have had and continue to have, go to www.nrdc.org.

☐ Research the charity before you give. Find a cause that you're passionate about—something that speaks to your heart. Just be sure that the charity to which you are giving your hard-earned dollars really uses the funds it collects to help the people or causes it's supposed to be helping. Keep in mind that charity is also big business, and that the administrative costs can eat up a huge percentage of charitable contributions. So, before you give, do some research and ask some questions. My favorite web site to research a charity is www.Charity Navigator.com. Others you can try include www. justgive.org, www. give.org, and www. guidestar.org.

☐ Commit to an amount. The practice of proactively giving back is called *tithing*. If you donate a set percent of your income on a regular basis, like each time you get paid, you will compile an impressive record of contributions. Select a percentage that feels right to you

and that you know you can manage. Once you've done that, make a commitment to donate that amount on an ongoing basis.

☐ Now make it automatic. The best way I know to give to a cause you truly believe in is to make the process automatic by arranging to have a percentage of your income automatically deducted from your paycheck or checking account and transferred to the charity of your choice.

☐ Find out if your donations are tax-deductible. Visit the IRS web site at www.irs.gov. Many organizations are recognized by the IRS as a bona fide tax-exempt charity under section 501(c)(3) of the Tax Code. Your income can be offset by as much as 50 percent, depending on the amount you give.

☐ Check out these other worthwhile green causes that need your help:

● GreenPeace (www.greenpeace. org)

● World Wildlife Fund (www.world wildlife.org)

● Earthday Network (www. earthday.net)

● EcoLogic Development Fund (www.ecologic.org)

● Global Green USA (www.global green.org)

☐ Visit www. finishrich.com to download a free chapter on giving back.

Carbon Offsets

IN THE EARLY PAGES OF THIS BOOK, YOU CALCULATED your carbon footprint. In the chapters you've read since, you've learned about the many ways you can reduce your carbon footprint. But it might not be possible for each of us to change *all* of our behaviors.

One thing you can consider to "make up for" your destructive behaviors is carbon offsetting. A carbon offset is a way of reducing emissions from one activity in order to make up for emissions you can't reduce from another. Carbon offsets make sense only if we use them for behaviors we can't avoid—rather than as a substitute for changes we can easily make. For instance, buying offsets doesn't make it okay to drive a Hummer!

There's really no such thing as a straight-up, one-for-one way to negate the impact of your action. But you can try to tip the balance in the right direction by helping fund projects aimed at curbing global warming.

GO GREEN ACTION STEPS

☐ Do your research. Many supposed carbon offsets are of questionable value—and several plans are under way to regulate the market so consumers know that what they're buying is truly helping the planet. A new organization called the Voluntary Carbon Standard helps evaluate carbon offsets, so you know your money is going to a legitimate endeavor. Learn about the VCS at www.v-c-s.org.

For a great primer on how to choose carbon offsets, what questions to ask, and what alternatives to consider, read Treehugger.com's guide "How to Green Your Carbon Offsets." Click on "How to Go Green" and then on the carbon offsets link.

☐ Consider purchasing renewable-energy certificates (RECs)—a type of carbon offset that helps subsidize renewable energy. Learn more about RECs, also called green tags, at www.green-e.org.

Get a Green Credit Card

THERE'S A REASON THAT THIS TIP IS IN THE "GIVE Green" section of the book. Simply put, a green credit card will not save you money. But it *can* offer rewards that let you help save the Earth.

Just as some credit cards let you earn frequent-flier miles, now "green cards" let you help the planet when you shop. The true impact comes from thousands of people using these cards so the benefits add up.

The first type of green credit card is one that comes with carbon offsets. Such cards invest a percentage of the purchases you make in emission-reduction efforts such as methane capture and reforestation.

OFFSET

eleven tons of CO_2 if you put $750 of your monthly purchases on your GE card.

If 100,000 people did that, it would be equivalent to taking 175,000 cars **OFF THE ROAD.**

Another option is the affinity card. For every set amount of money you spend, a small percentage is donated to the nonprofit that is associated with that card.

According to Bankrate.com, most of these cards charge an interest rate about 1 percent higher than those of regular cards—so you don't want to use them unless you can pay the full balance every month. And a green card is not a reason to consume more—that would be anti-green and not very smart.

GO GREEN ACTION STEPS

☐ Be honest with yourself. If you're overwhelmed by credit card bills, skip this tip and instead pick up one of my books in the FinishRich series to learn how to get out of debt (start with the *FinishRich Workbook* or *Start Late, Finish Rich*).

☐ Consider a card that offers carbon offsets. To learn more about GE's Money Earth Rewards card, go to www.myearth rewards.com. The card allows you to select both "carbon offsets" and "half cash back"—a nice flexible feature.

Bank of America just introduced the Brighter Planet Visa carbon-offset card (visit www. BrighterPlanet. com for details), where carbon offsets will be purchased through NativeEnergy. It is estimated that for every $1,000 spent on the card, one ton of carbon offsets will be purchased.

☐ Consider an affinity card, too. Bank of America issues many affinity cards, for organizations such as Defenders of Wildlife and the Humane Society. Go to www.bankof america.com/cred itcards for more information.

Wells Fargo lets you use reward points to support renewable energy. Go to www.wells fargorewards.com.

GIVE GREEN
Tip Nº 49

Join the Green Community

On July 7, 2007, concerned citizens across all seven continents joined together to deliver a worldwide call for action to solve the climate crisis. The event was called Live Earth—a series of worldwide concerts featuring over 150 musical acts in eleven global venues. The event united close to 2 billion fans, in person and via television, broadband, radio, and wireless platforms, as the global warming crisis took center stage.

When we join together with other like-minded people, the support, energy, and goals that we share propel us to achieve greater success than if we "go it alone." This is true in so many areas of life—and also when it comes to going green.

So don't go it alone! Harness the power of the crowd—or, at the very least, a small group with similar interests. Join an online community whose members are committed to living a greener lifestyle—you'll get inspired, learn from their successes and missteps, and be swept up in the spirit of community. Or create your own group, with friends, family, and neighbors—perhaps a book club whose theme is green—and get inspiration while learning incredible lessons about the world around you.

☐ Find out about green events taking place nationwide each April on Earth Day, and plan your own, at www.earthdaynetwork.org.

☐ Find your local posse online. Visit www.meetup.com and search on "green living." Try these sites, too:

● www.ecotreadsetters.com
The community for friends of the environment.

● www.makemesustainable.com
The MMS community is free to join and provides a virtual space for you to invite peers, share your actions, and encourage others to reduce their impact.

● www.razoo.com
Join the Razoo community, united with others to make a positive difference in the world. There you can also join a group to meet others with similar interests and shared visions.

● www.zaadz.com
Zaadz is a social networking site whose intention it is to provide an online sanctuary for personal development.

● www.care2.com
More than 8 million people have joined this site to discover, share, and take action toward living a greener life. It claims to be the largest online community of people passionate about making a difference.

☐ Check out sites that offer green news and support:

● www.treehugger.com Get informed, interact, and take action. Treehugger is one of the leading green sites out there. An amazing resource for all things green.

● www.Idealbite.com Subscribe to receive your daily green tip in your inbox.

● www.greendaily.com AOL's green site, offering news, stories, and resources.

● http://green.yahoo.com
Yahoo's green site, offering tools, news, blogs, and more.

● www.grist.org
Offers environmental news and commentary, including advice columnists and tons of hot topics.

☐ Connect with other green singles at:
www.greensingles.com.

www.planetearthsingles.com.

☐ Start a green book group. To access my recommended reading list of green books, visit www.greengreen.com/reading.

Vote Green

☐ Get involved locally. A great resource to find out what is happening in your state is the League of Conservation Voters (www.lcv.org). The majority of decisions on the environment—including land use, conservation, recycling, and energy efficiency—are made at the state and local levels and have a huge impact on the environment. Read your local paper and scan community

YOU HAVE THE POWER TO MAKE CHANGE. THE ENVIronment is an issue that impacts every single one of us, regardless of our geographic location. Our health, our economy, our national security all depend on the well-being of the planet. Your voice, vote, and support are needed to move this issue forward. Get started by learning more about environmental issues.

According to a 2006 Bloomberg/*Los Angeles Times* poll, 74 percent of Americans think that the government needs to take more action to fight global warming. But a *USA Today*/Gallup poll found that energy and the environment fall toward the bottom in the list of concerns that voters take into account when deciding where to place their vote.

I encourage you to make the environment a priority when selecting a candidate. It is important to learn about candidates' positions and voting records on environmental issues—at every level, from President of the United States right down to your city council members. Hundreds of cities around the country have passed climate-change legislation and are taking steps to reduce their emissions. Collectively, that will surely make a difference. States have also stepped up. At the beginning of 2007, more than half of U.S. states had taken action to fight global warming.

As I write this, at the federal level, Congress is considering several climate change–related bills but has yet to pass any major legislation. Getting in-

bulletin boards to find out about local environmental issues and events. Another great resource for information about the environmental positions of local candidates is your local chapter of the Sierra Club, which can be found at www.sierraclub.com.

☐ Vote for the environment. The 2008 election is crucial to the future direction of U.S. policy on climate change and the environment. Read up on candidates' positions and their environmental agendas. Go to www.grist.com to read interviews with every presidential candidate on their environmental policies. One federal law being considered is the Climate Security Act, also known as the Warner-Lieberman bill, which calls for mandatory emissions reductions and a cap-and-trade system for carbon emissions.

☐ Act globally. The United Nations Framework Convention on Climate Change (UNFCCC) has been bringing the world's governments together for thirteen years to develop international solutions to global warming—things like carbon trading markets and mechanisms for clean energy development. The UNFCCC led to the Kyoto Protocol, an emissions-reduction program that has been ratified by 174 countries. Stay up to date on the international effort to create a successor treaty at www.unfccc.int.

volved and showing your support will help encourage the federal government to act, both domestically and as part of the international response. *Did you know that the United States is the only developed nation not to ratify the Kyoto Protocol, a landmark international effort to curb emissions that change the climate?* It's time for our country to start playing a leadership role in building a global clean-energy economy.

A Final Word

I WROTE THE BOOK YOU HOLD IN YOUR HANDS BECAUSE I BELIEVE THAT each of us has the power to make a difference. I believe in my heart that most people are good and that the majority of us truly desire to do the right thing.

And I believe that as more of us are educated to be environmentally sensitive and eco-conscious, more of us will choose to make a difference by living a greener life.

As a result, we will help to turn the tide of global warming, we will live healthier lives, and we will prosper.

JUST DO "ONE GREEN THING"—BEGIN TODAY

The time to take action on the planet's health is now. We cannot afford to wait or debate. If we don't act now, not only will the planet suffer, but our kids and their kids will suffer, too.

So where will you begin? This book is filled with fifty tips, so you can choose what to do and when to do it. *The secret, however, is to start.* You don't need to do all fifty things. Just pick *one* tip, and do it. Do "One Green Thing"—and then tell a friend. I know that living greener for you and the planet will come from taking that first step. Once you start to live green, you won't ever go back.

Take that first step today. Then get selfish for a few minutes and consider the financial impact of your green change. How much could your one green thing save you this year? And if you invested that savings in a green investment or simply in your retirement plan or savings account, what would it be worth in ten, twenty, or thirty years?

Doing the math is simple. Go to www.greengreen.com and click on the Latte Factor Calculator. Take it for a test ride. See how going green can make your financial life greener, too.

Think about it. You're helping the planet, improving your health—and becoming richer. How green and great is that!

Please let us know about the "One Green Thing" (or more!) you did. Share your success story, and offer others your inspiration at www.green green.com. Or email your story to me at success@greengreen.com. Until we meet again, I hope you will enjoy your journey to a greener life.

Live Green and Live Rich!

DAVID BACH

Sources

GETTING STARTED: KNOW YOUR IMPACT

- **200 of the world's leading climate scientists:** 2007 Bali Climate Declaration by Scientists posted at the web site of the Climate Change Research Centre at the University of New South Wales, Sydney, Australia. www.climate.unsw.edu.au/bali/.

FIND YOUR LITTER FACTOR

- **Coffee cup facts:** Web site of Green Mountain Coffee Roasters and International Paper. www.ecofriendlycup.com/.
- **Fast Company article:** Charles Fishman, "Message in a Bottle," July/August 2007.
- **100,000 cars for a year:** Web site of Earth Policy Institute, "Bottled Water: Pouring Resources Down the Drain," by Emily Arnold and Janet Larsen, February 2, 2006. www.earth-policy.org/Updates/2006/Update51.htm.
- **96 percent of bottles are single servings, which have lower recycling rate:** Container Recycling Institute, Washington, D.C., "Water, Water Everywhere: The Growth of Non-Carbonated Beverages in the United States," by Jennifer Gitlitz and Pat Franklin, February, 2007. www.container-recycling.org/assets/pdfs/reports/2007-waterwater.pdf
- **9 out of 10 plastic water bottles are simply thrown away:** CNN.com, Rachel Oliver, "All About Plastic," September 16, 2007.

- **San Francisco ban:** San Francisco Chronicle, Cecilia M. Vega, "Mayor to Cut Off Flow of City Money for Bottled Water," June 22, 2007.
- **EcoShape bottle:** New York Times, Claudia H. Deutsch, "A Spotlight on the Green Side of Bottled Water," November 3, 2007.
- **FIJI Water:** New York Times, Claudia H. Deutsch, "For Fiji Water, a Big List of Green Goals," November 7, 2007.
- **Save $500 in a year by breaking a bottle-a-day habit:** Based on $1.39 for a 20-fl.-oz. bottle of Aquafina, buying one bottle a day for a year.

DRIVE SMART, FINISH RICH

- **Car ownership is second-highest household expense after shelter:** web site of U.S. Department of Labor, Bureau of Labor Statistics, "Consumer Expenditures in 2005," February 2007. www.bls.gov/cex/.
- **Automotive industry spending:** Web site of Public Citizen, "Auto Manufacturers Spend Billion Marketing SUVs to American Consumers," February 26, 2003. www.citizen.org.
- **241 million cars/trucks on the road in the United States:** U.S. Department of Transportation.
- **United States has 30 percent of the world's automobiles:** Washington Post, Sholnn Freeman, "Pollution in Overdrive," June 28, 2006.

We use 8.2 million barrels of oil a day, 11 percent of world consumption, more than Saudi Arabia produces each day: Web site of environmental defense. "Putting the Brakes on U.S. Oil Demand." John DeCicco with Rod Griffin and Steve Ertel, 2003. www.environmentaldefense. org/documents/3115_OilDemand.pdf.

Our cars produce 1,300 million tons of CO_2 each year: Web site of Union of Concerned Scientists, "Automakers pollute the press." www.ucsusa.org/ clean_ vehicles/avp/automaker-v-the-people-alliance-ad-fact-sheet.html.

INCREASE YOUR FUEL ECONOMY

Average U.S. fuel economy is 20.2 mpg: EPA, "Light-Duty Automotive Technology and Fuel Economy Trends: 1975 Through 2007." www.epa.gov/otaq/ fetrends.htm.

Average in Europe is 35 mpg: Wall Street Journal, "Can U.S. Adopt Europe's Fuel-Efficient Cars?" June 26, 2007.

All car fuel-economy numbers from web site of U.S. Environmental Protection Agency, Green Vehicle Guide, www. epa.gov/emissweb/.

Reduce CO_2 emissions by 6,420 pounds: assumes one gallon of gasoline combusted produces 20 pounds of CO_2.

UPGRADE TO A HYBRID

Car fuel-economy numbers from web-site of U.S. Environmental Protection

Agency, Green Vehicle Guide, www.epa. gov/emissweb/.

Save 8,340 pounds CO_2: Assumes a savings of 417 gallons of gasoline, by going from 20 mpg to 45 mpg. Assumes one gallon of gasoline combusted produces 20 pounds of CO_2.

GO BIODIESEL

Reduces emissions by 75 percent: National Biodiesel Board, Jefferson City, MO. "NBB Joins House Ag Committee in Rally for Renewable Fuels Standard," press release, December 5, 2007, posted at www.biodiesel.org.

Save more than five cents for every mile you drive; save 750 gallons of gasoline: Assumes driving 15,000 miles using gasoline at $2.75/gallon and 20 mpg versus biodiesel at $3.20/gallon and 38 mpg.

MAINTENANCE MATTERS

All savings calculations from U.S. Department of Energy and U.S. Environmental Protection Agency web site, "Keeping Your Car in Shape," www.fuel economy.gov/feg/maintain.shtml

Save up to $798 in gas every year and keep 5,800 pounds of CO_2 out of the air every year: Assumes one gallon of gasoline combusted produces 20 pounds of CO_2, 290 gallons of gas saved, $2.75/gallon.

GET RID OF A CAR

Average annual cost to own a midsize car,

driving 15,000 miles, is $8,580: web site
of American Public Transportation Association, Washington, D.C., "Automobile
Driving Costs, 2005," www.apta.com/
research/stats/fares/drivcost.cfm

- *If every family gave up a car, we'd reduce
emissions by 413 billion pounds:* Assumes
3,640 pounds per household. See below.

- *Keep 3,640 pounds of carbon out of
the air:* Assumes household savings of 70 miles per week, per City
of Seattle study, "*Way to Go Seattle!*
Final Results for One-Less-Car, 2002"
posted at http://www.seattle.gov/waytogo/
pdfs/5FinalResults2003v4.pdf. Assumes
one gallon of gasoline combusted produces 20 pounds CO_2, 20 mpg car.

SKIP A TRIP

- *91 percent of Americans commute to
work alone in their car:* U.S. Department
of Transportation, RITA, Bureau of
Transportation Statistics, "Highlights
of the 2001 National Household Travel
Survey." www.bts.gov/publications/high
lights_of_the_2001_national_household_
travel_survey/html/section_01.html

- *Average 30 miles round-trip:* U.S. News
& World Report, Kim Clark, "Career
Spotlight: New Benefit: Help with Com-
muting Costs," September 24, 2005.

- *We could save 149 million tons of emissions if everyone cut out one car trip a
week:* Assumes one 30-mile trip, 20
mpg, $2.75/gallon, 1,560 lbs CO_2, and
190,625,023 licensed drivers.

- *40 percent of all U.S. car trips are less
than two miles:* web site of Trek Bicycle
Corporation, www.1world2wheels.org/

- *Reduce your household emissions by 30
percent if one driver switched full-time
to public transit:* American Public
Transportation Association, Washington, D.C., "Public Transportation Use
Substantially Reduces Greenhouse
Gases, According to New Study," news
release, September 26, 2007.
www.apta.com/media/releases/070926_
climate_report.cfm

- *Denmark facts:* copenhagengirlsonbikes.
blogspot.com/

- *Save $215 a year:* See assumptions
above.

GET ENERGY SMART

- *Homes account for 20 percent of energy
demand:* Energy Information Administration, "Energy Consumption by Sector, 1949–2006," www.eia.doe.gov/emeu/
aer/txt/ptb0201a.html.

- *And produce 20 percent of CO_2 emissions:* EIA, "Emissions of Greenhouse
Gases in the United States 2005:
Executive Summary—Carbon," www.
eia.doe.gov/oiaf/1605/ggrpt/summary/
carbon.html.

- *Average home emits twice the CO_2 of the
average car:* Alliance to Save Energy,
"Saving Energy: Why Efficiency and
Why Now?" January 10, 2007.

- *Average home was 1,750 square feet in
1978, almost 2,500 square feet in 2006:*
U.S. Census Bureau, "Median and Average Square Feet of Floor Area in New
One-Family Houses Completed by Location," www.census.gov/const/C25Ann/
sftotalmedavgsqft.pdf.

- *In 1973, 25 percent of homes were less
than 1,200 square feet; today only 4
percent are:* Census Bureau, reported
in Idaho Statesman, "Environment at
Home: Smaller Houses Mean Lower
Utility Bills, Less Cleaning," February
26, 2007.

- *Today, 23 percent of homes are bigger
than 3,000 square feet:* CNNMoney.com,
Les Christie, "Honey, I Stretched the
House—Again," July 25, 2006.

- *The Solaire . . . uses 35 percent less:* www.
solaire.com. See also www.albanese.com.

GET AN ENERGY AUDIT

- *Changes you make as a result can save
you up to 30 percent:* U.S. Department
of Energy, Energy Efficiency and
Renewable Energy web site, "A Consumer's Guide to Energy Efficiency and
Renewable Energy." www.eere.energy.
gov/consumer/your_home/energy_audits/
index.cfm/mytopic=11170.

- *Average yearly costs of heating/cooling:*
Per Energy Information Administra-
tion, reported at CNNMoney.com, Steve
Hargreaves, "Home Heating Bills on the
Rise," October 9, 2007.

- *Reduce your CO_2 emissions by 9,515
pounds a year:* Assumes a 1,500-square-

foot home, 30 percent savings, total energy consumption of 23,652 kilowatt-hours, 1.341 pounds CO_2/kilowatt-hour.

RUN A TIGHT SHIP

- *Roughly half our energy expenses are from heating and cooling, which results in 150 million tons of CO_2 per year:* U.S. Department of Energy, Energy Efficiency and Renewable Energy, "Energy Savers: Tips on saving energy and money at home," www.eere.energy. gov/consumer/tips/heating_cooling.html.
- *Wrapping/sealing ducts can result in 20 percent efficiency increase:* Energy Star and U.S. Environmental Protection Agency, "Duct Sealing," October, 2004. Posted at www.energystar.gov.
- *Reduce your home's emissions by 2,808 pounds of CO_2:* Assumes a 1,500-square-foot home, 14,200 kilowatt-hours, 20 percent increase in efficiency, 1.341 pounds CO_2/kilowatt-hour.

GET GREEN ENERGY

- *85 percent of U.S. energy is from fossil fuels:* Web site of U.S. Department of Energy, Office of Fossil Energy, www. fossil.energy.gov/.
- *One million solar homes would keep 4.3 million tons of CO_2 out of the air a year:* TodayShow.com, "Nine Quick, Easy Tips to Help Save Mother Earth," June 29, 2007.

DO IT BY DEGREES

- *Adjusting your thermostat by 3 degrees on a 1,500-square-foot house saves $114 and 2683 pounds of CO_2:* Based on Department of Energy 2001 energy prices per square foot, from "Space Heating Energy Consumption and Expenditures by Square Feet and Usage Indicators, 2001," at www.eia. doe.gov/emeu/recs/recs2001/ce_pdf/ spaceheat/ce262u_sqft_useind2001.pdf; adjusted to reflect 43% increase in natural gas prices, according to Energy Information Administration. http:// tonto.eia.doe.gov/dnav/ng/ng_pri_sum_ dcu_nus_a.htm.
- *Every degree you turn it down in winter saves you 5 percent:* Web site of Pacific Gas and Electric Company, "Energy

Saving Tips," www.pge.com/res/energy_ tools_resources/tips/index.html.
- *Every degree you turn it up in summer saves you 3 percent:* Web site of California Energy Commission, Consumer Energy Center, www.consumerenergy center.org/tips/summer.html.
- *Programmable thermostat could save you $150 a year:* Energy Star web site, U.S. Department of Energy and U.S. Environmental Protection Agency, "Programmable Thermostats," www.energystar.gov/ index.cfm?c=thermostats.pr_thermostats.

UNPLUG IT

- *Phantom load accounts for 27 million tons of CO_2 annually and costs Americans $4 billion:* Rocky Mountain Institute, "Getting Savvy About Standby Power," November 2, 2007.
- *Could be 25 percent of your electric bill:* ScienceDaily.com, "Vampire Appliances Cost Consumers $3 Billion a Year, Says Cornell Energy Expert," September 27, 2002.
- *Phantom loads of cube transformers are 20 to 50 percent:* "Wind Turbine Considerations: Energy Conservation, Profitability and Ownership," Marie Powell, May 24, 2007, web site of Center for Rural Affairs, Lyons, NE, www.cfra.org/node/432.
- *Strip $94 off your yearly electric bills; reduce your home's emissions by 1,430 pounds of CO_2:* Assumes $938 average electricity bill (Energy Information Administration, www.eia.doe.gov/ emeu/recs/recs2001/ce_pdf/enduse/ce1- 1e_climate2001.pdf), 10 percent savings (based on 1996 U.S. average of five percent and 2004 California average of 15 percent), 10,656 kilowatt-hours saved (EIA "Residential Energy Consumption Survey," www.eia.doe.gov/emeu/recs/ recs2001/detailcetbls.html).

BE AN ENERGY STAR

- *ENERGY STAR saved Americans $14 billion and the greenhouse gas equivalent of 25 million cars in 2006:* U.S. Environmental Protection Agency, "EPA Climate Programs Prevent Greenhouse Gas Emissions and Save Dollars," press release, September 26, 2007.

Washer cost savings and water savings: Web site of Energy Star. U.S. Environmental Protection Agency and U.S. Department of Energy, "Save Money, Energy and Water — Choose ENERGY STAR Qualified Clothes Washers," www.energystar.gov.

Plasma vs. LCD TVs: *Wall Street Journal*, "That Giant Sucking Sound May Be Your New TV," December 13, 2007.

SWITCH TO CFLS

Wal-Mart info: "Wal-Mart Surpasses Goal to Sell 100 million compact fluorescent light bulbs three months early," press release, Bentonville, Arkansas, October 2, 2007. Posted at web site of Wal-mart. www.walmartfacts.com/articles/5328.aspx.

CFLs use 75 percent less electricity and last 10 times longer: Web site of Energy Star. U.S. Environmental Protection Agency and U.S. Department of Energy, "Compact Fluorescent Light Bulbs," www.energystar.gov.

Save $45 over the lifetime of a bulb: Assumes $5/year energy savings per ENERGY STAR CFL savings calculator and nine-year lifetime per package information of some bulbs.

Reduce carbon emissions by 67 pounds of CO_2: Assumes 75 percent energy savings (see above), or 50 kilowatt-hours per bulb.

PLANT TREES

Can reduce wall and roof temperatures in summer by 20 to 40 degrees: Xcel Energy, Inc., Eau Claire, WI, "Smart Energy Guide," 2005, posted at www.xcelenergy.com/docs/retail/SmartEnergyGuide.pdf.

Can save you $100 to $250 over a year: Based on 1500 to 2500 square foot home, Department of Energy 2001 energy costs per square foot, updated to reflect 2006 energy prices.

Save $177 on energy costs; reduce your home's emissions by 3,952 pounds: Assumes 1500 square foot home.

GO LOW FLOW

2 gallons wasted per minute while brushing teeth: U.S. Environmental Protection Agency, EPA WaterSense, "Indoor water use in the United States," July 2007, www.epa.gov/OW-OWM.html/water-efficiency/docs/ws_indoor508.pdf

5 to 10 percent of U.S. homes lose 90 gallons of water a day through leaks; less than 1 percent of water is available for human use: Web site of U.S. Environmental Protection Agency, EPA WaterSense, "Statistics and Facts," www.epa.gov/watersense/news/facts.htm

Water shortages in 36 states by 2013: Web site of U.S. Environmental Protection Agency, EPA WaterSense, "Water Supply and Use in the United States, www.epa.gov/watersense/pubs/supply.htm

TURN OFF THE TAP

Toilet uses most water in your home: Web site of U.S. Environmental Protection Agency, EPA WaterSense, "High-Efficiency Toilets," http://www.epa.gov/WaterSense/pubs/het.htm.

Save $72 a year just in your bathroom, and conserve 9,200 gallons of water: Assumes switching to a low-flow showerhead, installing a dual-flush toilet (not including cost of toilet), and turning off the tap while brushing teeth.

GROW A GREENER LAWN

Seven billion gallons of water a day used on landscaping, 1/3 of residential usage, up to half is wasted: Web site of U.S. Environmental Protection Agency, EPA WaterSense, "Outdoor Water Use in the United States," www.epa.gov/WaterSense/pubs/outdoor.htm.

Longer lawn requires less water; grass clippings hold in moisture: Web site of U.S. Environmental Protection Agency, "Tips for a Waste-Free Lawn and Garden," www.epa.gov/osw/specials/funfacts/may.htm.

Lawn mowers emit as much pollution in an hour as a car does in 100 miles; Mowers use 800 million gallons of gas —a year: Web site of People Powered Machines, www.peoplepoweredmachines.com/faq-environment.htm and Ideal Bite tip library, "Reel and Electric Mowers," www.idealbite.com/tiplibrary/archives/making_the_cut_lawnmowers.

We spill 17 million gallons refueling them: Gardener's Supply Company, Better Gardening Bulletin, Number 4, Burlington, Vermont, posted at web site of U.S. Environmental Protection Agency, www.epa.gov/otaq/consumer/f96o18.pdf, and *E/The Environmental Magazine,* LuAnne Roy, "Buzz Cut: Electric Lawn Mowers Beat the Gas Guzzlers at Their Own Game," September/October 2007.

Electric mowers cost $5 a year to run: *E/The Environmental Magazine* (see above).

Save 67 million pounds of chemicals: Animal Welfare Institute, "Endangered Species Handbook," 2005. Posted at http://www.endangeredspecieshandbook. org/projects_lawns.php.

BUILD GREEN

Majority of Americans say they'll pay more for green homes: McGraw-Hill Construction, "Residential Green Building SmartMarket Report," June 1, 2006.

Home values increase by $20 for every $1 in annual energy savings: Residential Energy Services Network, www.natres net.org/ratings/mortgages/default.htm.

60 percent of all trees logged domestically are for homes; average 2,000-square-foot home requires an acre's worth of wood: Dan Chiras, *The New Ecological Home,* Chelsea Green, 2004.

Average home uses 17 tons of concrete: National Association of Home Builders, cited in "Small Is Beautiful: U.S. House Size, Resource Use, and the Environment." *Journal of Industrial Ecology,* winter/spring 2005.

Concrete is made from cement, which produces 5 percent of global greenhouse gases: *New York Times,* Elizabeth Rosenthal, "Cement Industry Is at Center of Climate Change Debate," October 26, 2007.

Twice as many homes use vinyl siding as any other material: "U.S. Census Bureau Statistics show twice as many homeowners side their homes with vinyl than with any other material." From "About Vinyl Siding," posted at the web site of the Vinyl Siding Institute, www.vinylsiding.org/aboutsiding/.

Vinyl is toxic: U.S. Environmental Protection Agency, Technology Transfer NetworkAir Toxics web site, Hazard Summary—created in April 1992; revised in January, 2000, entry for vinyl chloride. epa.gov/ttn/atw/hlthef/vinylchl.html.

BUY IN BULK

Can save you up to a third: Shiloh Farms, interview.

Containers and packaging make up 31 percent of municipal solid waste, 80 million tons in 2006: U.S. Environmental Protection Agency, "Municipal Solid Waste Generation, Recycling, and Disposal in the United States: Facts and Figures for 2006," November, 2007, posted at www.epa.gov/epaoswer/non-hw/ muncpl/pubs/msw06.pdf.

BRING YOUR BAGS

500 billion to 1 trillion plastic bags used worldwide each year, and up to 30 billion end up as litter: John Roach, "Are Plastic Grocery Bags Sacking the Environment," *National Geographic News,* September 2, 2003, www.news. nationalgeographic.com.

Cities considering bag bans: Ian Urbina, "Pressure Builds to Ban Plastic Bags in Stores," *New York Times,* July 24, 2007.

Save $44 a year: Assumes 100 billion plastic bags used in the United States, 882 per household; assumes a 5 cent discount for each one you don't use.

Ireland has saved 18,000,000 liters of oil since 2002, reducing production of plastic bags by 90 percent: "The PlasTax: About Ireland's Plastic Bag Tax," www. reusablebags.com.

EAT LESS MEAT

Methane from captive livestock accounts for 18 percent of global greenhouse gases: Brad Knickerbocker, "Humans' Beef with Livestock: A Warmer Planet," *Christian Science Monitor,* February 20, 2007.

2006 study: G. Eshel and P. Martin, "Diet, Energy and Global Warming," *Earth Interactions,* vol. 10, March 2006, pp. 1–17.

Amazon cleared mainly to grow beef: D. Kaimowitz et al., "Hamburger Connection Fuels Amazon Destruction," Center for International Forestry Research.

- **Pound of beef vs. pound of wheat:** www.chooseveg.com/conservation.asp.
- **Pound of beef vs. pound of potatoes:** David de Rothschild, *The Live Earth Global Warming Survival Handbook*, Rodale/Melcher Media, 2007.
- **Calorie of animal protein vs. calorie of vegetable protein:** www.goveg.com/environment-globalwarming.asp.
- **Save at least $6 on your weekly grocery bill:** Based on half a pound of ground beef per person for four people vs. one serving of lentils per person for four people.
- **Reduce 1.4 billion tons of animal waste:** Jim Motavalli, "The Case Against Meat," *E/The Environmental Magazine*, January/February 2002.

GROW YOUR OWN
- **Food travels an average of 1,500 to 2,500 miles to our plates:** Brian Halweil, "Worldwatch Paper #163: Home Grown: The Case For Local Food In A Global Market," Worldwatch Institute, 2002, www.worldwatch.org/node/827.

USE RECYCLED PAPER PRODUCTS
- **Save $39.53 by switching to recycled:** Based on 20,805 sheets/person, $41.61 for Seventh Generation vs. $81.14 for Charmin.
- **We could all save 19 million trees:** Based on Seventh Generation savings statistics and assuming 13 four-packs of 400 sheets.

CLEAN GREEN
- **Average U.S. household spends $600 a year on cleaning supplies:** U.S. Bureau of Labor Statistics.
- **Average U.S. household uses 40 pounds of chemicals a year:** Mike Paquet, "Clean Homes, Clean Waves," *Making Waves*, February 2000, Surfrider Foundation, www.surfrider.org/makingwaves/makingwaves16-1/4.html.
- **Chemical cleaning supplies are an $18 billion industry:** Ilana DeBare, "Cleaning Up Without Dot-Coms," *San Francisco Chronicle*, October 8, 2006.

THE BEAUTY OF GOING GREEN
- **Average U.S. household spends $600**

a year on personal-care products: U.S. Bureau of Labor Statistics.
- **Many standard ingredients are potential carcinogens or hormone disrupters:** Lisa Stiffler, "Putting On Your Face Could Cause Ugly Health Problems," *Seattle Post-Intelligencer*, November 6, 2006.
- **2002 United States Geological Survey study on hormones and other contaminants in our waterways:** Kimberlee K. Barnes, et. al., "Water-Quality Data for Pharmaceuticals, Hormones, and Other Organic Wastewater Contaminants in U.S. Streams, 1999–2000," U.S. Geological Survey, 2002, www.toxics.usgs.gov/pubs/OFR-02-94/.
- **Study of 23,000 cosmetic products:** Richard Wiles, letter to the FDA, "Cosmetics with Banned and Unsafe Ingredients," September 26, 2007, Environmental Working Group, www.ewg.org/node/22610.

GREEN YOUR DECOR
- **We spend $78 billion a year on home furnishings:** Elisabeth Leamy, "When Buying Furniture, Don't Always Trust the Tags," *ABC News*, November 20, 2006.
- **Harmful chemicals in furniture:** Susan Fornoff, "What's in Furniture: It's Enough to Make You Sick," *San Francisco Chronicle*, October 24, 2007.

PROFIT BY RECYCLING
- **690,000 tons of waste:** Municipal Solid Waste, "Municipal Solid Waste Generation, Recycling, and Disposal in the United States: Facts and Figures for 2006," Environmental Protection Agency, www.epa.gov/epaoswer/non-hw/muncpl/pubs/msw06.pdf.

BUY AND SELL EVERYTHING
- **$52 billion worth of items on eBay:** "eBay Marketplace Fast Facts," eBay, September 30, 2007, http://news.ebay.com/fastfacts_ebay_marketplace.cfm.
- **$210 per user:** Based on 248 million users, per "eBay Marketplace Fast Facts," eBay, September 30, 2007, http://news.ebay.com/fastfacts_ebay_marketplace.cfm.

PAY AS YOU THROW

- *75 to 90 percent of trash is recyclable:* www.earth911.org and www.ecocycle.org.
- *United States produces more than a third of the world's waste:* "Solid Waste and Landfills," A Recycling Revolution, www.recycling-revolution.com/recycling-facts.html.
- *4.5 pounds per person per day, more than half to landfills:* Municipal Solid Waste, "Basic Information: Municipal Solid Waste (MSW)," Environmental Protection Agency, www.epa.gov/msw/facts.htm.
- *United States emits more methane than any other source:* Methane, "Methane: Sources and Emissions," Environmental Protection Agency, www.epa.gov/methane/sources.html.
- *Landfills leak toxic materials:* Scott C. Christenson and Isabelle M. Cozzarelli, "The Norman Landfill Environmental Research Site What Happens to the Waste in Landfills?", August 2003, http://pubs.usgs.gov/fs/fs-040-03/.
- *Trash facts on aluminum cans:* "Eco-Facts 2004," Eco-Cycle, www.Ecocycle.org.
- *Save $26 a year by "paying as you throw":* Based on several local case studies.
- *PAYT keeps 6.5 million tons from landfills annually:* Lisa A. Skumatz, Ph.D., and David J. Freeman, "Pay As You Throw (PAYT) in the US: 2006 Update and Analyses," Environmental Protection Agency, December 30, 2006, www.epa.gov/epaoswer/non-hw/payt/pdf/sera06.pdf.

GET RID OF JUNK MAIL

- *$160 billion in catalog purchases in 2006:* Based on a study by the Direct Marketing Association, "Catalog Sales Growth Continues to Outpace Overall Retail Growth," 2001, http://retailindustry.about.com/library/bl/q2/bl_dma060401a.htm.
- *Sears sends more than 425 million catalogs:* Forest Ethics, http://forestethics.org/section.php?id=158.
- *Average adult gets 41 pounds of junk mail a year:* 41pounds.org, www.41pounds.org/.
- *Average adult is on 50 mailing lists:* RecycleWorks, "Reduce Residential Junk Mail," www.recycleworks.org/junkmail/residential.html.
- *Save $1,413 on catalog purchases:* Per person based on $160 billion.
- *Save 100 million trees a year:* Native Forest Network, www.nativeforest.org/stop_junk_mail/nfn_junk_mail_guide.htm.

GREEN YOUR BABY

- *No difference in impact between cloth and disposable diapers:* U.K. Environment Agency study, reported by BBC News, "No Green Winner in Nappy Debate," May 19, 2005.
- *$40 a week on infant formula:* "Cost of Having a Baby," Sure Baby, www.surebaby.com/costs.php, and review of prices on Amazon.com.
- *PBDEs and infant death:* www.healthy-child.com/cribdeathcause.htm.
- *Save 600 glass jars:* Cheryl Tallman and Joan Ahlers, "Homemade Baby Food: A Fresh Start to Healthy Eating," Keep Kids Healthy LLC, http://www.keepkidshealthy.com/experts/nc/homemade_baby_food.html.

GREEN YOUR PET

- *3 to 4 million homeless pets euthanized every year:* Humane Society of the United States.
- *Low-quality ingredients in pet food:* Dr. Larry Siegler, "What You Need to Know About Your Pet's Food," Only Natural Pet Store, www.onlynaturalpet.com/KnowledgeBase/knowledgebasedetail.aspx?articleid=4&Keywords and "Get the Facts: What's Really in Pet Food," The Animal Protection Institute, updated May 2007, http://www.api4animals.org/facts.php?p=359&more=1.
- *Americans spent $38.4 billion on pets in 2006:* Press Release, "Pet Spending at All-time High," American Pet Products. Manufacturers' Association, March 23, 2006, www.appma.org/press_releasedetail.asp?id=84.

GET OUTDOORS

- *700 million acres of public land in the United States:* "Public Lands, Recreational Opportunities and Natural

Resources," Environmental Protection Agency, www.epa.gov/climatechange/effects/publiclands.html.

GREEN YOUR HOLIDAYS

- *$2.7 billion on gift wrap:* Donna Garlough and Lauren Sanders, "Eco Gift Wrap," *Body + Soul*, November/December 2006, www.marthastewart.com/portal/site/mslo/menuitem.3a0656639de6 2ad593598e10d373a0a0/?vgnextoid=d649 35ea97ea4110VgnVCM1000003d370a0aR CRD&vgnextfmt=default.
- *300,000 trees harvested annually to produce holiday cards:* New Leaf Quarterly, Winter 07/08, posted at www.newleafquarterly.com/NLQFall07web.pdf

GO GREEN AT WORK

- *$4.3 billion in energy and 32 million tons of CO_2 could be saved by turning off office lights and computers:* Sun Microsystems, "New Poll Reveals 73 Percent of U.S. Workers Want Employers To Be Environmentally Responsible But Lag In Their Own Efforts To Help," press release, Santa Clara, CA, August 1, 2007, posted at www.sun.com.

BRING YOUR LUNCH TO WORK

- *1.8 million tons of trash a year from takeout food packaging:* Mother Jones, "The Doggie Bag Dilemma," November/December 2006.
- *A quarter of all litter in New Jersey is from takeout packaging:* Californians Against Waste, "Unrecycleable Takeout Food Packaging," posted at www.cawrecycles.org/files/fpo_brochure.pdf.
- *Americans spend over $134 billion a year on fast food:* Eric Schlosser and Charles Wilson, *Chew On This: Everything You*

Don't Want to Know About Fast Food, Houghton Mifflin, 2006.

GREEN YOUR COMPUTER

- *Shut down eight power stations and avoid 7 million tons of CO_2:* www.earth911.org.

DO IT ONLINE

- *Save 18.5 million trees, 2.2 billion tons of greenhouse gases, and 1.7 billion pounds of waste if we all got electronic statements:* James Van Dyke, Javelin Strategy and Research, Pleasanton, CA, "Why Electronic Billing and Banking Is Good for the Nation's Environmental Health," posted at www.electronic payments.org/pdfs/EnvironmentalImpactsStudy_09-19.pdf.
- *Save $400 or more on stamps and late fees:* Average credit card late fee is $34.42, average of 12.7 credit cards per household.

THINK BEFORE YOU PRINT

- *Paper accounts for more than a third of municipal solid waste:* Ecocycle.org, "Eco-Facts 2004."
- *Spare 18-60 pounds of pollution for every 40 cases of recycled paper:* NRDC.

TELECOMMUTE

- *Two days per week lets you drive 3,000 fewer miles, save $430, and eliminate 3000 pounds of CO_2:* Assumes 30 miles per trip, 50 weeks of the year, 20 mpg, 20 pounds of CO_2 per gallon of gasoline.
- *95,000 tons of perc used each year in the United States and Canada:* Web site of Worldwatch Institute, Washington, D.C., "Dry Cleaning," www.worldwatch.org/node/4131.

BE A GREEN BUSINESS TRAVELER

- *Air travel is less than 5 percent of emissions:* Slate.com, "Jet Green?" October 2, 2007.
- *U.S. aircraft emissions expected to increase 65 percent by 2025, triple by 2050; greenhouse gases from aircraft are exacerbated by altitude:* Environmental News Network, "EPA Urged to Cut Pollution from Aircraft," December 5, 2007.
- *Aviation is fastest-growing source of emissions:* CNN.com, "All About: Planes," November 6, 2007.
- *From 1990 to 2004, CO_2 from flying doubled:* Responsibletravel.com, "Flying in the Face of global warming—to fly or not to fly?" www.responsibletravel.com/Copy/Copy101993.htm.
- *18% of travel is for business:* Fairfield County Business Journal, "Business Travel Up, Finally," May 16, 2005
- *Continental's sustainability initiatives:* Fortune.com, "10 Green Giants," http://money.cnn.com/galleries/2007/fortune/0703/gallery.green_giants.fortune/2.html.
- *Virgin Atlantic's sustainability initiatives:* Web site of Treehugger, "Virgin Atlantic testing Bio-fuel on Jumbo Jet," by Matthew Sparkes, October 16, 2007, www.treehugger.com/files/2007/10/virgin_atlantic.php and ABC News Online, "Branson plans cuts to plane emissions," September 28, 2006, www.abc.net.au/news/newsitems/200609/s1750607.htm.
- *EU planning to reduce airplane carbon emissions:* Environment News Service, "States, Groups Demand Aircraft Climate Emission Limits," December 6, 2007.
- *Marriott's sustainability initiatives:* Web site of Marriott, www.marriott.com/marriott.mi?page=environmental Initiatives.
- *For every mile you fly, .6 pounds of CO_2 emitted:* Kockelman et al., "Travel Choices and Their Relative Contributions to Climate Change," www.ce.utexas.edu/prof/kockelman/public_html/TRB08ClimateChange.pdf.

INVEST GREEN

- *SRI has $2.3 trillion invested in it:* Social Investment Forum, "2005 Report on Socially Responsible Investing Trends in the United States," January 2006, posted at www.socialinvest.org/areas/research/trends/sri_trends_report_2005.pdf.
- *Goldman Sachs is investing $1.5 billion in green companies:* Christopher Wright, Ecosystem Marketplace, "Goldman Sachs Expects Big Returns from Going Green," posted at GreenBiz.com, www.greenbiz.com/news/reviews_third.cfm?NewsID=34521.
- *CalPERS and CalSTRS are investing more than $1 billion:* Emily Thornton and Adam Aston, with Justin Hibbard, *BusinessWeek*, "Wall Street's New Love Affair," August 14, 2006, www.businessweek.com/magazine/content/06_33/b3997073.htm?chan=top+news_top+news.

VOTE GREEN

- *2006 Bloomberg/Los Angeles Times Poll:* Kim Chipman, "Americans Want More Federal Action on Environment, Poll Says," August 4, 2006, www.bloomberg.com www.bloomberg.com/apps/news?pid=washingtonstory&sid=aQ84QNxiL.AM.
- *USA Today/Gallup poll:* www.usatoday.com/news/politics/election2008/2007-12-04-poll_N.htm.

Acknowledgments

PUTTING THIS BOOK TOGETHER WAS TRULY A LABOR OF LOVE, AND I HAVE so many people to thank for their dedication and commitment to making it happen.

First to Liz Dougherty, my trusted friend and right hand on all of my writing projects. This is the seventh book you have worked on with me since 2002 (just amazing). You have always been there to oversee every book project from start to finish. This time you gave more than 110 percent, and for that I am forever grateful. Without you, this book would simply have not been possible, nor would it be as fantastic and heartfelt as it is. Thank you from the bottom of my heart.

To Hillary Rosner, my coauthor: You're a true champion for the cause, and your expert guidance along the way has been invaluable. I sincerely thank you for working so hard on this project. And to our researcher, Jimmy Hague: Thank you for your commitment and for a job well done!

To my team at Doubleday Broadway Publishing Group: This project was not without its challenges, but I thank you all for sticking with it and believing in the core mission. To Stephen Rubin, Michael Palgon, and David Drake: I thank you for your valuable insight and commitment from beginning to end. To my Editor Extraordinaire, Kris Puopolo: Without you, this book would not have been published, and I thank you for all of your hard work, expert guidance, invaluable feedback, and tireless devotion to the very end. And to all of the Broadway Team who worked so hard on this book, including: Jean Traina, John Fontana, Erin Mayes, Elizabeth Rendfleisch, Catherine Pollock, Judy Jacoby, Louise Quayle, Rachel Horowitz, Kim Cacho, Chris Fortunato, and Rebecca Holland—thank you!

To my literary agents, Suzanne Gluck and Jay Mandel, at William Morris Agency: Thank you for all of your support and help in getting this project off the ground. I'm looking forward to a great partnership for many years to come! Thanks for all you do.

To my attorney and friend, Stephen Breimer. Thank you for always looking out for me with such care and attention to detail.

Thank you to my team at FinishRich Media: Liz Dougherty, Elisa Garafano, Elizabeth O'Gorman, Nicola Zahn, and Vanessa Rudin.

And to my family: Marty and Bobbi Bach, Emily Bach, and Michelle Bach—your love and support means the world to me. And last but certainly not least—to my little son, Jack. I hope in some small way this book will make a difference in the amazing life you're destined to live on this beautiful planet. I hope you'll always know how much your Dad loves you.

DAVID BACH
New York, 2008

TO DAVID BACH FOR INSPIRING A BETTER WORLD; JAY MANDEL FOR making this book happen; Kris Puopolo and Liz Dougherty for constant invaluable insight; Jimmy Hague, researcher extraordinaire; the Carbon, Climate and Society Initiative brain trust; Larry Kirshbaum for unwavering support; Bernie and Ethel Rosner, who taught me to live by my values; and Philip Higgs, who makes everything worth it: Thank you.

HILLARY ROSNER
Boulder, Colorado, 2008

Index

About David Bach

David Bach HAS HELPED MILLIONS OF PEOPLE AROUND THE WORLD take action to live and finish rich. He is the author of seven consecutive national bestsellers, including two consecutive #1 *New York Times* bestsellers, *Start Late, Finish Rich* and *The Automatic Millionaire,* as well as the national and international bestsellers *The Automatic Millionaire Homeowner, Smart Women Finish Rich, Smart Couples Finish Rich, The Finish Rich Workbook,* and *The Automatic Millionaire Workbook.* Bach carries the unique distinction of having had four of his books appear simultaneously on the *Wall Street Journal, BusinessWeek,* and *USA Today* bestseller lists. In addition, four of Bach's books were named to *USA Today's* Best Sellers of the Year list for 2004. In all, his FinishRich Books have been published in more than fifteen languages, with more than five million copies in print worldwide.

Bach's breakout book *The Automatic Millionaire* was the #1 business book of 2004, according to *BusinessWeek.* It spent fourteen weeks on the *New York Times* bestseller list and was simultaneously number one on the bestseller lists of the *New York Times, Business-Week, USA Today,* and the *Wall Street Journal.* With over a million copies in print, this simple, powerful book has been translated into twelve languages and has inspired thousands around the world to save money automatically.

Bach is regularly featured on television and radio, as well as in newspapers and magazines. He has appeared six times on *The Oprah Winfrey Show* to share his strategies for living and finishing rich. He has been a regular contributor to CNN's *American Morning* and has also appeared on CNN's *Larry King Live,* ABC's *The View,* NBC's *Today* and *Weekend Today* shows, CBS's *Early Show,* Fox News Channel's *The O'Reilly Factor,* CNBC's *Power Lunch,* CNNfn, and MSNBC's *The Big Idea with Donny Deutsch.* He has been profiled in numerous major publications, including the *New York Times, BusinessWeek, USA Today, People, Reader's Digest, Time, Financial Times,* the *Washington Post,* the *Wall Street Journal, Los Angeles Times, San Francisco Chronicle, Working Woman, Glamour,* and *Family Circle.* He is a featured contributor and columnist with *Redbook* magazine and on Yahoo!, where his column "The Automatic Millionaire with David Bach" appears bi-weekly.

David Bach is the creator of the FinishRich® Seminar series, which highlights his quick and easy-to-follow financial strategies. In just the last few years, more than half a million people have learned how to take financial action to live a life in line with their values by attending his Smart Women Finish Rich®, Smart Couples Finish Rich®, and Find The Money Seminars, which have been taught in more than two thousand cities throughout North America by thousands of financial advisors.

A renowned motivational and financial speaker, Bach regularly presents seminars for and delivers keynote addresses to the world's leading financial service firms, Fortune 500 companies, universities, and national conferences. He is the founder and Chairman of FinishRich Media, a company dedicated to revolutionizing the way people learn about money. Prior to founding FinishRich Media, he was a senior vice president of Morgan Stanley and a partner of The Bach Group, which during his tenure (1993 to 2001) managed more than half a billion dollars for individual investors.

As part of his mission, David Bach is involved with many worthwhile causes including serving on the board for Habitat for Humanity New York and cofounding Makers of Memories, a charity organization dedicated to helping women and children who are victims of domestic violence.

David Bach lives in New York, where he is currently working on his tenth book, *Fight for Your Money*. Please visit his web site at www.finishrich.com.

About Hillary Rosner

Hillary Rosner WRITES ABOUT THE ENVIRONMENT AND SCIENCE FOR many national publications. She contributes frequently to the *New York Times* and her work has appeared recently in *Popular Science, Men's Journal, Audubon, Seed,* and *Town & Country.* She holds a master's degree in environmental studies from the University of Colorado, where she received a three-year National Science Foundation fellowship to study climate change. Hillary contributed to Al Gore's bestselling book *An Inconvenient Truth,* as well as to the *Live Earth Global Warming Survival Handbook.* She has been a senior editor at the *Village Voice* and a contributing editor at *New York* magazine. She lives in Boulder, Colorado, with her husband, Philip Higgs.

NEW!
Are you ready to finally
STOP WORRYING ABOUT MONEY?
Discover...
FINISHRICHcoaching
Change your life with 1-on-1 financial coaching from a trained specialist
Breakthrough coaching program offers:
• Personalized mentoring focused on specific solutions
• Motivation and encouragement to help you stay on track
• Accountability and support to help you accomplish your goals
"I've designed this program to ensure you...Finish Rich!"
— #1 New York Times Bestseller David Bach
Ready to learn more about this breakthrough new program?
Call or visit us online and register for a free 30 minute consultation.
VISIT www.FinishRich.com
OR
CALL 1-866-602-3625
(mention code BACHGG)

About This Book

WATERKEEPER®ALLIANCE